Acclaim for
Essential Monastic Wisdom

"Benedictine Hugh Feiss has rendered a valuable service in introducing the *Essential Monastic Wisdom* to what I suspect will be a large and appreciative audience. Aimed primarily at non-monastics, though not exclusively, the author backs up his own writing on the various components of the monastic way with quotations from the best of ancient and modern Christian monastic authors."

> —Patrick Hart, O.C.S.O., Abbey of Gethsemani,
> general editor of the *Journals of Thomas Merton*

"Contemplative wisdom shimmers through these pages. What a jewel of a book for those who see the beauty of the monastic way, but must find the cloister amidst the demands of family and freeway, the marketplace and the mundane."

> —Michael Downey, author of *Trappist*

"Hugh Feiss's well-chosen selections will help open up the riches of the Christian monastic tradition to readers from all walks of life."

> —James A. Wiseman, O.S.B., associate professor
> of theology, The Catholic University of America

"There are periods of history in which religion contributes very little to larger society, and there are periods in which religion holds it all together. Hugh Feiss's collection of 'monastic wisdom' reveals healthy and happy religion at its best. Not just wisdom, but readable, practical, and hopeful spirituality."

> —Fr. Richard Rohr, O.F.M., Center for Action
> and Contemplation, Albuquerque, NM

"For the many seeking a deeper spiritual life, this book beautifully presents insights, selected from centuries of monastic wisdom, that are a guide for daily living."

> —Jeffrey Burton Russell, University of California
> at Santa Barbara, author of *A History of Heaven*

"Hugh Feiss, O.S.B., reflects the insights of one who has lived the experience of the sages of the Christian monastic tradition. His introductions to virtuous communal living—unassuming yet honest—invite the reader to linger over and to savor old favorite sayings and recently translated excerpts, as well as new expressions of rediscovered monastic values from current writers. Monastics and those interested in Christian monasticism will find a treasury of wisdom from which to draw both old and new riches for their lives."

> —Mary Forman, O.S.B., president,
> American Benedictine Academy

"For someone like me who dos not usually like anthologies . . . this is a very satisfying book. Hugh Feiss is one of the most learned monks in America, and he has drawn wonderful things from his storehouse of quotes from the early and medieval periods. Much of this material has not been translated, much less gathered into a popular anthology. He has gathered it into the right categories and introduced each section with insightful comments."

> —Fr. Terrence G. Kardong, O.S.B.,
> author of *Benedict's Rule*

"Father Hugh Feiss's culling of sources gives us not only an interesting witness to the perennial value of monastic practices but fruitful insights as to how they can enrich our lives today. This is a volume most useful to those who want the radiance of the monastery to illumine their path, its practices to be a reality in their daily journey."

> —M. Basil Pennington, O.C.S.O.

"A rare and timely insight into a world often fraught with mystery for the lay person—the world of the monastic. A wonderful resource, simple and comprehensive, offering ordinary folks a unique opportunity to draw upon and integrate into their own lives the treasures of monastic wisdom."

> —Edwina Gately, author of *I Hear a Seed Growing*

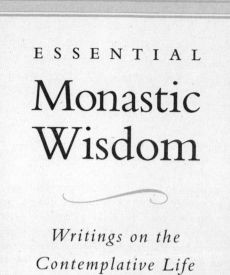

ESSENTIAL
Monastic
Wisdom

*Writings on the
Contemplative Life*

Edited, Translated, and Introduced by

Hugh Feiss, O.S.B.

FOREWORD BY

Kathleen Norris

HarperSanFrancisco
A Division of HarperCollinsPublishers

Permission acknowledgments appear on page 219,
which constitutes a continuation of this copyright page.

HarperCollins books may be purchased for educational, business,
or sales promotional use. For information please write: Special Markets Department,
HarperCollins Publishers Inc., 10 East 53rd Street, New York, NY 10022.

HarperCollins Web site: http://www.harpercollins.com
HarperCollins®, 📖®, and HarperSanFrancisco™
are trademarks of HarperCollins Publishers Inc.

FIRST HARPERCOLLINS PAPERBACK EDITION PUBLISHED IN 2000

Library of Congress Cataloging-in-Publication Data

Essential monastic wisdom : writings on the contemplative life / edited,
translated, and introduced by Hugh Feiss. —1st ed.
p.   cm.
Includes bibliographical references.
ISBN 0–06–062483–3 (cloth)
ISBN 0–06–062482–5 (pbk.)
1. Benedictines—Spiritual life. 2. Monastic and religious life.
3. Christian life-Catholic authors. I. Feiss, Hugh.
BX3003.E88 1999
255'.01—dc21   98–49369

00 01 02 03 04 ❖RRD(H) 10 9 8 7 6 5 4 3 2 1

Contents

Acknowledgments

Some of the key ideas in this book originated in a conversation with Abbot Celestine Cullen, O.S.B., president of the Annunciation Congregation of Benedictines. He probably doesn't remember the conversation, but talking to him helped me sort out my ideas. I have Kathleen Norris to thank for suggesting that I might be the one to write a book such as this. Kathleen and I first met when we both went to the wrong place for a concert. She has been doing kindnesses to me ever since, not the least of which is her foreword to this book. I owe thanks also to the late Ambrose Zenner for material I used from his dissertation on Benedictine peace. Tom Grady kindly acted as my agent and guide in the unfamiliar world of publishing. Marilyn Hall was theological consultant, friend, and proofreader; I needed all three. I am grateful to my editors, John Loudon, Karen Levine, Terri Leonard, and Carl Walesa, at Harper San Francisco for their patience with an aging novice. The book is dedicated in gratitude to my parents and to Father Bernard Sander, O.S.B., all of whom have by my calculations spent collectively 165 years teaching me by word and example. In particular, I owe to Fr. Bernard my strong conviction that the cloister of the monastery is not primarily a barrier but a meeting place where monks and others can encourage one another on the journey to God and to human wholeness.

Foreword

by Kathleen Norris

This book constitutes an excellent guidebook to the literature of monasticism, a guide I searched for in vain when I first encountered the Benedictines some fifteen years ago. Now the general reader, as well as the one who is seeking to enrich an understanding of monasticism, can benefit from Fr. Hugh Feiss's prodigious reading in the monastic tradition, as well as his many years of experience as a Benedictine monk. Fr. Hugh is one of those rare scholars who have a gift for assimilating obscure material in such a way as to make it accessible and relevant to the contemporary reader. In this book he has more than fulfilled his desire to spark "a conversation between some interesting monastic authors and contemporary people who might like to meet them."

Among the lively characters whose words enliven this book are Amma Syncletica, a wise and fierce fifth-century nun, who sounds quite up-to-date when she observes that "towards women generally there is great hostility in the world." Writing with great poignancy about the suffering of women in childbirth—it was a major cause of death for women in the ancient world—she reminds monastics not to become puffed up with piety, nor to look down on people outside the monastery walls. We meet Benedict, author of the monastic rule that has served Benedictines well for over fifteen hundred years, and find him bested by his sister in an argument. We encounter the twelfth-century monk and biblical commentator Peter of Celle stating that a room without reading is "a hell without consolation . . . a tomb without ventilation." The wisdom of Hildegard of Bingen rings through these pages along with that of the thirteenth-century nun Gertrude the Great, who was but one of the remarkable nuns of the monastery of Helfta. Among the twentieth-century writers we find not only the well-known American monk Thomas Merton but Esther de Waal, a British Anglican who has generated an interest in monastic spirituality and practice among many Protestants.

Spirituality is a well-known buzzword, but I think it is safe to say that this book will help people to understand better the seventeen-hundred-year-old branch of Christian spirituality known as monasticism. Originally a lay movement, it has flowed through those many centuries as an underground stream, at times running counter to the fancy trappings of Christendom, at times corrupted by them, at times surfacing like a pure, cold drink to refresh the faith of ordinary Christians. It has always allowed for contradiction, leaving plenty of room for the imaginative and the mystical, even as it remains solidly grounded in orthodox theology and a disciplined way of life.

One of the intriguing things about this book is that Fr. Hugh does not offer a dry chronology, but has organized his citations around the nonnegotiables of Benedictine life, such as prayer, work, and hospitality. He also examines lesser-known practices and values, including reading, communication, mutual support, and leadership, peppering his commentary with asides that reveal a great deal about contemporary monastic life. Monasteries are not immune to the ills of society, and Feiss comments that for today's American Benedictines, work and workaholism are threatening the traditional balance of monastic life. It is a spiritual issue, he insists, a matter of character, as "in the end we are judged by who we have become, rather than what we have accomplished."

The trust that is essential for human life has taken a beating in our time, and Fr. Hugh returns us to a basic understanding that "we are life and death for each other." The mutual support that a monastery (or a family, for that matter) requires is a rare commodity, but as Feiss reminds us, it is an essential part of Christian faith. "If a person is not properly related to one's neighbors," he writes, "that person is not properly related to Christ." Over the centuries, the trials of community life have inspired Benedictines to much impassioned commentary, and some marvelously sound advice. When another person angers you, writes the sixteenth-century monk Louis de Blois, "regret that your heart is bitter and ask for God's help."

The stereotypical monk is given to silence, but Fr. Hugh makes it clear that in a monastery, even silence is made to serve the value of peaceable interpersonal relations. In one of the most striking passages in the book, he sums up the monastic life as "a training in the art of listening, which begins in silence, develops in attentiveness, and is perfected in communication." People who visit monasteries often comment on how well they are listened to. That stands out, because for most of us the art of careful listening is drowned out by the sheer noisiness of our everyday lives: television, faxes, Muzak, busy free-ways, and airwaves. But with characteristic Benedictine insight and humility, Feiss remarks that "the principal enemy of interior and ex-terior silence for most of us is our own tongue."

Fr. Hugh and the writers he has cited in this book make it clear that monastic spirituality is not a romantic venture, but a demanding, daily practice, and that its wisdom is based on a practical and humane understanding of human beings. The monastic men and women quoted here can offer anyone, no matter what his or her religious be-liefs—or lack thereof—sensible, useful, and sometimes even beauti-ful insights into what it means to live and love more deeply, striving for peace with oneself and one's neighbor. The twentieth-century Benedictine Joan Chittister, writing on the subject of humility, really sums up one of the central goals of monastic life, and a goal accessible to anyone, when she speaks of the importance of retaining "a proper sense of self in a universe of wonders."

Introduction

This book aims to tap into the practical wisdom of the seventeen-century-old monastic tradition. A selection of short texts from Christian monastic authors arranged by topic and prefaced by introductory essays invites readers to ponder what the men and women of this tradition have learned about how to be integral human beings who live peacefully and reverently in their place and time with their comrades and their God. The book is written primarily for those who are not monks, but in the hope that even monks might learn something from the texts and ideas presented here.

The reader will find these pages divided into three parts: ordering time and place; character; and the good desired and possessed. The first section studies how Benedict arranged the day, dividing it into three regularly scheduled activities—work, prayer, and reading—but making provision for interruptions arising from the needs of colleagues or guests. In the second part of the book, the longest, the chapters present eleven character traits that the Benedictine monastery tries to inculcate in its members. The third section looks beyond order and character to two passions that give them life and purpose: longing and love.

Although this book is not addressed specifically to Catholics or Christians, no effort has been made to hide the Christian matrix of Benedictine monasticism. My conviction is that a rich and reasonable human life will have certain characteristics, whatever the religious convictions of the reader. This book queries an ancient tradition for guidance about how to live sanely. For this reason, one should look here not for a complete picture of Benedictine life, but for an exposition of those features of Benedictinism that seem likely to be of interest and inspiration to people living in the world of today. Hence, the reader will look in vain for a discussion of topics peculiar to monks or Catholicism—for example, the Eucharist or celibacy.

Christian monasticism emerged in the third century in various parts of the Mediterranean world. Although monks of later centuries would look to Antony (ca. A.D. 251–356) and Pachomius (ca. A.D. 292–346) as founders, they were not the first monks. The deeds and sayings of many desert fathers *(abbas)* and mothers *(ammas)* were gathered in oral and written collections. The rules and traditions governing many Christians experimenting with a solitary life (hermits or anchorites) and celibate community (cenobites) were also handed on. Most of these early monks were not members of the clergy, and, then as now, most of the clergy (deacons, priests, and bishops) were not monks.

In the sixth century, the *Rule of Benedict* synthesized the teachings of these pioneer traditions. It drew particularly on the writings of Cassian and a strange document called the *Rule of the Master*. The *Rule of Benedict* gradually became the dominant monastic rule in the West. It enjoyed something close to a monopoly from the time of Charlemagne until the twelfth century.

In 909–910 the monastery of Cluny was founded in Burgundy. Subject only to the papal authority and free to elect their own abbot, the monks of Cluny developed customs that were adopted by many others monasteries. Cluny stressed private and liturgical prayer. Under Hugh, who served as abbot from 1049 to 1109, the influence of Cluny was at its zenith; hundreds of monasteries emulated its way of life. Some of those monasteries were subject to the abbot of Cluny, while others retained their own abbots. Monks of Cluny were mainstays in the renewal efforts that swept the church in the latter half of the eleventh century; some of them were elected pope. There were also other monastic reform centers, such as Hirsau and Gorze, and only a minority of Benedictine monasteries ever affiliated with Cluny.

In the twelfth century there were many new experiments in eremitical and cenobitic Christianity. Some of the resulting innovative orders, such as the Cistercians, followed the *Rule of Benedict*. Spreading out from the abbey of Cîteaux, founded in 1098 near

Dijon, the Cistercians had by the end of the century founded hundreds of monasteries. As an instrument of uniform observance and mutual assistance, the Cistercian founders produced the Charter of Charity. Their monasteries were connected to each other by filiation, so that the abbot had the right and duty to visit those monasteries founded by his monastery to make sure that observance in the daughter houses was up to standard. Moreover, the abbots of all the houses were supposed to meet annually in general chapter at Cîteaux. The statutes of the general chapters became the law of the order. Thus there emerged the first full-blown religious order in the church, even though the abbots of individual houses retained some autonomy and monks joined individual houses and not the order as a whole. The Cistercian Order had an immense flourishing in the twelfth century, as did the traditional Benedictines and the new canons regular, who followed the *Rule of Saint Augustine* but for the most part adapted the customs of Cluny or Cîteaux.

Throughout the monastic age, from Charlemagne until the end of the twelfth century, there were monasteries of women also. Sometimes these shared a superior with a house of men; sometimes they were established near a house of men or incorporated into an association of monasteries (like the Cistercians or Cluniacs) that included men's and women's houses; sometimes the women's communities were independent of juridical bonds with men's houses. In that case, an abbess might arrange to have a chaplain sent from a men's community or might hire the services of a priest or small community of priests. However, it was more difficult for women's communities to support themselves, so they were not as numerous as men's communities.

Tentatively in the twelfth century and explosively in the thirteenth, Christians went beyond the *Rule of Benedict* and the practices spelled out in the monastic customaries (detailed guides to observance) to explore new forms of religious life. Orders emerged that abandoned the Benedictine emphasis on the local community. Instead of joining a single monastery, a candidate joined a province, within which he could be moved about at will by his superiors. The provinces of these religious orders had several layers of government and connected the individual communities to the entire order and its superior general. Of these new orders, two of the most numerous and durable are the Dominicans and Franciscans. The Franciscans emphasized voluntary poverty; the Dominicans were especially dedicated to preaching. The male members of both orders are called *mendicants* or *friars;* there were also Augustinian, Carmelite, and Servite friars. For several centuries the female members of these orders lived much like the Benedictine nuns of earlier ages; in fact, enclosure was gradually made stricter during the later Middle Ages. Women who did not want to be enclosed nuns or were unable to find a place in a monastery developed the alternative of becoming Beguines, less strictly organized semireligious women who lived in towns, supported themselves by working, and lived and prayed together.

Meanwhile, during the thirteenth and fourteenth centuries the older monastic tradition represented by the Benedictines foundered. At the urging of the papacy, Benedictine monasteries were organized into congregations, which provided for mutual visitation and support. However, in most cases monks continued to join a single monastery, and the general chapters and visitators had only limited powers to interfere in the life of individual monasteries. There were various efforts at renewal within the Benedictine and Cistercian families, some of which were quite successful. Ludovico Barbo (1381–1443), John Trithemius (1462–1516), and Louis de Blois (1506–1566) were among the leaders of those reform movements.

About half the monasteries in Europe were closed at the time of the Reformation. Meanwhile, many new orders arose in the church, many of them dedicated to particular apostolic tasks, such as the education of the poor, the care of the sick, and missionary outreach. Their members usually did not live in large communities, but rather in small groups who worked together at a particular apostolic endeavor. Many did not say the traditional liturgy of the hours, which was a primary concern of the *Rule of Benedict*. The most important of these new orders was the Society of Jesus. Some women tried to develop similarly mobile and ministry-directed orders, but met with resistance from churchmen who insisted on enclosure for women's communities.

In seventeenth-century France, Benedictine life revived in the Congregations of Saint-Vanne and Saint-Maur. The Maurist Congregation had a superior general who resided in Paris. The priors of the individual houses were appointed to one-year terms. The houses were divided into six provinces, each of which had its own visitator and council, its own novitiate and house of studies, but members could be moved anywhere in the congregation. New members benefited from a solid seven-year program of studies. The scholars of the congregation published editions of the writers of the early church, monastic authors, and a literary history of France. The Maurists were a very diverse group, which varied from monastery to monastery and province to province. They produced many forceful personalities, of whom Jean Mabillon (1632–1707) was perhaps the greatest. Their theological outlook was nourished by Cartesian currents as well as by Thomism, but its main inspiration was the early Christian writers.

Armand-Jean le Bouthillier de Rancé (1626–1700), who became an adversary of Mabillon, a Benedictine, over the question of which studies were suitable for monks, initiated a reform movement among the Cistercians. By the time he was ten years old, de Rancé held several religious houses *in commendam,* including the Cistercian Abbey of La Trappe. From these houses he was entitled to a certain income. Theoretically, in return he was to be their protector. de Rancé went on to become a distinguished classical scholar, a graduate of the Sorbonne, and a priest. He led a worldly life, but the death of an older woman whom he had known since childhood led to his conversion. He gave away all his ecclesiastical holdings except La Trappe. He invited the Strict Observance of the Cistercian Order to take over the abbey in 1662. He made a year's novitiate at another abbey and then was appointed abbot of La Trappe in 1664. There he enforced a very strict discipline. Almost miraculously, the community of La Trappe survived the French Revolution under the leadership of Abbot Augustin de Lestrange (elected abbot in 1794). In 1893 the Trappists were recognized as a new, separate order called the Cistercians of the Strict Observance, or Reformed Cistercians. The order inherited a strongly penitential bent from de Rancé and Lestrange, as well as an emphasis on uniform observance.

Most of the Benedictine and Cistercian monasteries that survived the Reformation were closed during the French Revolution and its aftermath. By 1840 or so, there were very few monasteries, and in many areas of Europe all religious orders were outlawed. The revival of religious life after 1840 was almost miraculous. Many new orders were founded, especially for women, and for the next 150 years members of these women's orders, some of which adopted the *Rule of Benedict,* rendered enormous service to the church as teachers, nurses, intercessors, and models of dedication to God. Monastic communities following the *Rule of Benedict* flourished as well, and by 1990 there were more than thirty thousand Benedictine and Cistercian monks and nuns. However, their number had been falling since around 1965. The reasons for the decline are many, and may have more to do with the plan of God than human choice.

As the number of men and women in monasteries declines, the number of people interested in the monastic tradition seems to be increasing rapidly. As a result, the family of most monasteries consists of a core of vowed men and women inside the cloister and a larger number of associates who live outside the cloister but look to the Benedictine tradition for guidance in leading their Christian lives in the secular world. They find that this ancient and resilient tradition has something to teach men and women of all walks of life about how to live wisely and joyfully, how to budget time, how to get along together, how to walk gently on the earth. This book presents to a wider audience some of the values these associates (some of who are formally connected to a monastery as lay oblates) find in the Benedictine tradition.

The writings chosen to represent the Benedictine monastic tradition are eclectic. The quotations in each chapter are arranged in chronological order. Four pre-Benedictine sources are cited: Antony and Pachomius, the titular founders of anchoritic and cenobitic monasticism; the desert fathers and mothers; and Syncletica, a woman monastic who lived around A.D. 400. Next, the *Rule of Benedict* is cited extensively; I have also included several selections from Gregory the Great's account of Benedict's life. The first representative of the tradition after Benedict is Bede, a renowned Anglo-Saxon monk and scholar, whose sermons are quoted a number of times. He is followed by Wulfstan of Worcester, a monk and bishop from eleventh-century England; again, it is from his life that I quote. The great monastic movement led by Cluny is represented by Abbot Hugh, a French contemporary of Wulfstan.

The twelfth century was probably the golden age of Christian monasticism. It is represented here by Anselm of Canterbury, Bernard of Clairvaux, Peter of Celle, and Hildegard of Bingen. From the late thirteenth century comes Gertrude the Great, a nun who is claimed by both Benedictines and Cistercians. The next three centuries are represented by didactic and legislative works by three Benedictine abbots: Ludovico Barbo, John Trithemius, and Louis de Blois (Blosius), each of whom was touched by the reform impulses that enlivened Christendom in the period 1350–1600. From the seventeenth century, I have quoted from Jean Mabillon, a great Benedictine scholar.

The twentieth century is represented by the Trappist Thomas Merton and by two women each of whom has cast fresh light on the *Rule of Benedict* both for Benedictines and for men and women who are not monks but who are interested in monastic spirituality. Esther de Waal and Sr. Joan Chittister have both written commentaries on the *Rule of Benedict,* and it is from those that I quote; de Waal, a married woman and member of the Church of England, speaks for all those in married life and in other Christian traditions who have discovered Benedictine spirituality.

Those who would like to know more about the writers whose works are drawn from here should consult the biographical sketches at the back of the book. Also included there is a short bibliographical essay detailing the sources I have used and indicating some related reading.

There are certain subjects I have deliberately avoided. Celibacy is one. I am writing primarily for people who have no intention of being lifelong celibates, and monastic writers have not been very much interested in the theology of marriage. In fact, the authors I have studied do not seem to have been particularly preoccupied with celibacy either. There are also aspects of the Benedictine rule and tradition that seem outdated or of little relevance to non-monastics: the arrangement of the office, the penalties inflicted for coming late to services, and so forth. I have tried to select themes that are both prominent in the tradition and meaningful to me, in the hopes that these same topics will be helpful to others today as well.

I have never been an abbot or any other kind of monastic official in or out of my monastery. Moreover, by measures of the *Rule of Benedict,* I am a beginner. I have no desire and no right to tell people how to live. In fact, I have a deep suspicion of people who are confident that they know what is good for other individuals, because so often they seem to cross the line between telling and controlling. All I wish to do is facilitate a conversation between some interesting monastic authors and contemporary people who might like to meet them. My qualifications are a broad and long and occasionally deep acquaintance with the writings of the monastic tradition; forty years of struggling to live in that tradition; familiarity with many different monasteries, male and female; and a sympathy for my fellow inhabitants of late twentieth-century America.

I have tried to use inclusive language, both in my translations and in my own writing. Occasionally, it seemed best to alternate between masculine and feminine pronouns.

In writing this book, I was primarily concerned with the goals of monastic practices, what sort of persons Benedict wanted the people in his monastery to become. It is very difficult to properly evaluate practices, customs, and observances. Looking at them, as this book does, from the three angles I described earlier—the primary uses of time, the construction of character, and desire and love for the good—might help monastics appreciate the meaning and purpose of some of the things they customarily do. It might also suggest that the same purposes could be better achieved by doing things differently than in the past. As the book says, discernment is hard-won, and only after trial and error.

PART ONE

Ordering Time and Place

V ISITORS ARE ALMOST ALWAYS impressed by the order that characterizes monastic life. The monks and nuns walk quietly through the cloister precincts. They walk two by two to solemn liturgies. Each member of the community has an assigned place and assigned duties. It all seems to run like clockwork.

Some of this order appears to be a fairly modern invention as far as Christian monastic history goes. Benedict said nothing about marching two by two into church, though he certainly did value decorum. One can theorize—justifiably, I think—that orderly communities tend to attract personalities for whom order is a high priority, so that order almost becomes a religious norm, if not a religion, to which freer spirits are forced to conform. This irritated Thomas Merton. There is, he commented in *Contemplation in a World of Action*,

> a fatal tendency to dramatize the monastic life. A special costume and decor. A unique behavior, . . . a ritual solemnity and obsequiousness. In the end this amounts to attachment to feudal anachronism, and the monk who pretends to justify himself by these masks is only convincing people that he is an object for the museum.

Nevertheless, some kind of order is clearly necessary and important. Community life requires ordering. It is important to know who is doing the cooking today, what time we say morning prayer, who will get the mail, and so on. It is even important that we observe certain standards of polite behavior, just to avoid irritating those closest to us.

Even in one's individual life there needs to be order. It may not be necessary that I make my meditation every day at the same time or that I read Scripture a half hour a day instead of three and a half hours a week, but it is necessary that there be some sort of plan whereby I set aside time to do the activities to which I am committed. Left to chance, some of those activities will not get done.

How structured life should be depends in part on personality and circumstance, but structured it must be.

Benedict was legislating for a community of people who evidently were ethnically and educationally diverse. There were children and old men, monks who had transferred from elsewhere, priests and laymen. He needed to integrate this diverse cross section of humanity into a kindly, well-organized community so that everything would be done at the proper time. He achieved this integration through several mechanisms, the most important of which were seniority and the daily order, or horarium. Seniority meant that each member of the community was assigned a place that depended on the time of his or her arrival. All the members of the community had a place of their own. They knew where they belonged. Some tasks were assigned in rotation on the basis of seniority; others were assigned according to talent and skill.

More important for us was the horarium. Benedict divided the day into three principal activities: work, prayer, and reading. The details varied according to the season of the year, but the division left four to five hours for work, about three hours for prayer, and slightly less than three hours for private reading (there was also public reading in the dining room during meals and elsewhere in the interval between supper and compline). Benedict specified when the members of the community should be occupied with these activities. He also made provision for two other activities: hospitality toward guests and mutual help and support. These two activities could be required at any time and were unpredictable. In order to be hospitable and helpful to each other, the monks had to have some flexibility in their schedules. If their schedules were completely full and unalterable, and thus no time was available to be hospitable and helpful, those schedules needed to be changed.

Saint Benedict did not like idleness, but he does not seem to have assigned any of these activities simply as a remedy for idleness. Work, prayer, and reading were activities to which his monks were obligated by their calling, talents, and humanity, and if they devoted themselves to those activities zealously, they would not be idle. But the value of work, prayer, and reading far exceeded their contribution to keeping the monks from idleness.

In fact, in the prologue and elsewhere, the *Rule of Benedict* conveys a sense of urgency: one must hasten and run toward the goal of everlasting life. The goal is precious; there is no time to waste getting there.

Each of these five activities of the horarium will be discussed later. What is important here is the fact that there had to be time for hospitality and for mutual help and support. Saint Benedict teaches a very important truth here, a truth most of us know but often neglect to act upon: after God, other persons are the most important realities in our lives. If we are too busy to make time for people who need us, whether they are strangers or neighbors, there is something wrong with our priorities. Worse yet, we may be using our obligations to work and prayer (and perhaps reading) as an excuse to try to evade our obligation to be helpful and hospitable.

These five activities not only divided up the hours of the monks' day; they also correlate to the defined space of the monastery. Prayer was done in church, reading in the cloister (and later in the library or the cell), work in the workshops; hospitality was provided in the guest house; and mutual support was given wherever it was needed.

Beyond these five activities, other, basic human needs—for sleep, food, personal hygiene, and so forth—had to be accommodated. For sleeping there was a dormitory (and later private rooms); for eating, the dining room or refectory with a lectern for the reader; for hygiene, toilets and a place to wash; for the sick, an infirmary; for beginners or novice monks not yet fully integrated into the community, a novitiate. As time went on, monasteries added other rooms not specified in the *Rule,* but needed for conversing (parlor), for meeting (chapter room), and, once monasticism moved to northern Europe, for warming people (calefactory).

Thus time and space were divided and ordered, so that members of the community could live together in harmony, welcome guests, meet unexpected needs within the community, and individually fulfill those daily activities that were the basis of the monks' life, a life whose goal was to lead each member of the community to life everlasting.

The schedules for days and weeks varied somewhat with the seasons and the availability of sunlight. For monastics the most important temporal cycle was the annual liturgical cycle centered on Easter. This cycle fitted the story of Christ to the annual cycle of the seasons. It put the stamp of the mystery of birth and death, the paschal mystery, on the praying and reading, on the eating and fasting, on the consciousness of each monk. For each bit of dying to self there was the promise of resurrection; for each surrender, the promise of freedom.

Underlying all this concern for order, one senses a deep respect for the order of the universe, the harmony of the spheres, the beauty of the heavenly Jerusalem. Medieval monks spoke of the cloister using metaphors of heaven, of paradise, of the garden enclosed in the *Song of Songs.* In this they echoed the longing Benedict had for order and predictability in a world that was constantly threatened by chaos. His own career was evidence enough of the tumultuous times in which he lived. Monte Cassino, his last, best attempt at founding a monastery, was destroyed in 581 and several times afterward, but each time it arose from the rubble, and there monks once again sought to order their lives and their world for and with God.

Everything will be done at the proper time.

RULE OF BENEDICT

Idleness is the enemy of the soul, and so monks should be occupied at some times with manual labor, and at certain times with holy reading.

RULE OF BENEDICT

If you are hastening toward the heavenly homeland, with
Christ's help carry out this minimal rule for beginners, and
then with God's protection you will arrive finally at the
greater heights of doctrine.

    RULE OF BENEDICT

See to it that your private exercises are organized to be performed regularly. Prescribe for yourself what you will do
and when, and what things you want to be doing, but in
such a way that if sometimes obedience or some other reasonable cause or emergency requires it, you may abbreviate
any of your exercises, or even omit them, without inordinate worry.

    LOUIS DE BLOIS,
    MIRROR FOR MONKS

The monk renounces a life of agitation and confusion for
one of order and clarity. But the order and clarity are not
his own making; nor are they, so to speak, an institutional
product, an effect of exterior regularity. They are the fruit
of the Spirit.

    THOMAS MERTON,
    CONTEMPLATION IN A WORLD OF ACTION

After a few days of newspapers and reflection on their con-
tents [the author had been in the hospital], I am convinced
that what we need above all, and seem to have lost, are the
following: First we need to recover the belief that order is
possible, and that it rests with us to preserve it. Then we
need to desire to do this. . . . If, today, genuine order has become incredible it is because people are not fully capable of
experiencing themselves as persons with sufficient dignity
and responsibility to contribute to an order in which all are
fully and personally concerned.

    THOMAS MERTON,
    CONJECTURES OF A GUILTY BYSTANDER

To have a place to stand is a basic human need in order that I know where I belong, and it is necessary both in relation to the places and to the people in my life. It means, above all, that I have time and space for listening to the Word of God in all the many ways that God is reaching out to me. That will be totally impossible if I am always running, late, distracted, feeling ajar and torn apart. Benedict is helping me to find my own center. . . . Respecting boundaries, not letting things drift, means that I am totally present to whatever I am doing, present with awareness, and therefore with energy for whatever that place, that moment may bring me.

ESTHER DE WAAL, *A LIFE-GIVING WAY*

The Benedictine is clean, simple, and proper to the time and place because the stewardship of the universe demands a commitment to order, harmony, and rightness if it is to survive.

SR. JOAN CHITTISTER, *THE RULE OF BENEDICT*

CHAPTER I

Prayer

Saint Benedict was not a theorist about prayer, its nature, forms, and stages. On the other hand, he valued prayer very highly. He organized the liturgy of the hours or divine office very minutely, assigning psalms and other prayers to each of the seven daytime offices—lauds, prime, terce, sext, none, vespers, and compline—and the night office that his monks chanted or recited each day. He legislated that his monks spend more than three hours a day reading or listening to reading. He expected this reading to be prayerful and to lead to spontaneous or wordless prayer. Finally, he assumed that various monks would be moved to solitary prayer during the day, and he sought to make sure the oratory would be quiet and so suitable for such prayer. Benedict wanted reverent and frequent prayer, but he did not legislate any particular postures or breathing techniques. To those preoccupied with techniques, Benedict's teaching is something of a disappointment. Of course, he did recommend Cassian highly, and Cassian's *Institutes* contains a good deal of guidance about prayer, even suggesting a version of the Jesus Prayer.

Benedictine prayer is less about technique than it is about perseverance and attentiveness. Anyone who reads the Bible in a reverent, faith-filled manner or who attends carefully to the words of the liturgy of the hours will think about the application of what she reads and hears to her own life. Her reflection (meditation) will suggest changes in her behavior or cast new light on the teachings of the faith. Such reflection will then lead her to prayer: praise to God for his wondrous truth, thanks for his gifts, sorrow for her failures, and requests for forgiveness and help. If a person perseveres in such reading, reflection, and prayer, she will eventually find words less necessary, or even a hindrance, and she will simply rest in the presence and love of God. This, at least, is the way medieval monastic authors describe the development of prayer, from reading and recitation *(lectio divina)*, through reflection *(meditatio)* and prayer *(oratio)*, to contemplation *(contemplatio)*. In fact, this fourfold schema appears several times in the readings selected here.

Benedictine authors show a predilection for this kind of prayer, rooted in the communal or private reading of the Bible and related works. However, monastic authors never felt a need to confine their discussion of prayer to this traditional schema. In each age, monks learned new ways to structure prayer from the wider church. This is especially obvious in the writings of the Ludovico Barbo, John Trithemius, and Louis de Blois, all of whom lived between 1380 and 1560, and so were heavily influenced by the *Devotio moderna,* and especially Thomas à Kempis (1390–1471). This movement, which was centered in the Netherlands but was echoed elsewhere in Europe, emphasized methodical meditation techniques that served to guide reflection. These methods helped focus the mind on the topic of meditation.

Nevertheless, for the Benedictine, prayer is never primarily a matter of technique. It is the natural outflow from the heart of a believer nourished by the Word of God in the Scriptures and the liturgy. God has spoken; the Benedictine listens and answers with words, with actions, with silence.

During Benedictine history, there have been times when there were exaggerations about prayer. In many places, liturgical prayer was expanded beyond the generous limits allotted it by Saint Benedict as masses and additional offices and prayers were added to the daily horarium. This was somewhat self-defeating, since private reading, one of the two essential fonts of Benedictine prayer, was curtailed. Work was also curtailed, and so the monks became liturgical specialists, expected to pray on behalf of others. Insofar as this was thought to relieve others of the duty to pray, it was a manifest error. For the monks, it was also the destruction of the delicate balance and order that Benedict envisioned. One can imagine that this overemphasis on liturgical prayer ultimately led to a distaste for that very liturgical prayer, a rather specific sort of *akedia* or spirit of tedium regarding the things of God.

Another difficulty, more subtle perhaps, is that the concentration on ornate liturgical prayer tended to attract onlookers. Monastic prayer was no longer a model and encouragement for others to prayer, not an invitation to enter into prayer themselves, but a spectacle they watched. Saint Bernard thought he detected in the ornate churches of Benedictine monasteries a sort of come-on to pilgrims and benefactors who were attracted more by glitter than by grace. Insofar as people come to watch monks do splendid liturgies today, there is still a danger that performance for onlookers will contaminate the purity of monastic prayer. The way to avoid the problem is to encourage visitors to join in the prayer, not watch it. This danger of praying before others can also stain private prayer. Wulfstan solved that problem by having a hidden prayer room in each of his manor houses.

Prayer becomes difficult when we are preoccupied. If lack of time for surprise guests is a sign that our schedule is too full, then lack of concentration at prayer is a sign that our minds are too cluttered. Either we have too many distracting concerns or we need to learn how to loosen the grip that legitimate concerns have on our minds and imaginations. At times, however, distractions and difficulties in concentration are beyond our control. Then, Blosius says, we should patiently and cheerfully pray as best we can, trusting that God is pleased with our effort.

When there is just no time to set aside to pray because one's children require constant attention (a friend said that her one attempt to pray lauds after her son was born took four hours, with interruptions for nursing, changing, burping, etc.), or deadlines have to be met, or a family member is sick, Benedict's idea of spacing prayer times throughout the day (liturgy of the hours) needs adapting. The prayers will be rushed and silent, no more than an offering or a request for strength, but they can still be woven into the fabric of the day. The goal of regular prayers at appointed intervals is to "pray always," to draw the mind explicitly to God at regular intervals so that the rest of the time one can attend prayerfully to work, reading, brothers and sisters, spouses and children, guests and strangers. Short, hurried prayer like this will do for a while, but over the long haul abiding in the presence of God requires more time and concentration than we can give it at our busiest moments.

Saint Gertrude suggests that occasionally each nun should set aside a day for prayer, when she simply praises and thanks God. In the circumstances of modern life, when there are so many demands on our time and attention, such quiet days are all the more necessary. Everybody should have some noise-free, news-free place where she can spend a day or an hour in quiet, with God and with herself. There are many retreat centers and religious houses and parks where one can go for some quiet hours.

Ultimately, prayer is a means to and an expression of self-offering to God, a surrender of one's life and activities into God's hands. One can offer God splendid liturgy, daily meditation, competence in esoteric contemplative techniques, but none of this means anything unless one can surrender oneself. Second, prayer is meant to be a part of life. One brings one's activities and concerns to times of prayer; one slips short prayers into the intervals that occur in working and walking and weeding. In the end, prayer is about awareness of the divine presence, and that presence is everywhere.

A brother said to Abba Antony, "Pray for me." The old man answered him, "I will not have mercy on you, and neither will God if you yourself do not make an effort and if you do not entreat God."

ANTONY, *SAYINGS*

But if Pachomius prayed about someone's health and was not granted his request by the Lord, he was not surprised or afflicted at not being heard, for he knew the purpose toward which the saints tended. And he said in his prayer, "May your will be done, not mine" [Lk 22.42]. For he who is one with the Father in all things taught us that it ought to be so.

LIFE OF PACHOMIUS

There is a sadness that is helpful and a sadness that is destructive. It is a function of the useful sorrow, then, to lament about one's own sins as well as the ignorance of one's neighbors, but also to avoid falling away from one's purpose and to achieve the goal of goodness. These concerns, therefore, are the signs of a sorrow that is legitimate and good. There is also another kind of sorrow, prompted by the Enemy, which knows how to merge with the first kind. For he himself imposes a sorrow, completely irrational, which by some has also been called *akedia*. This spirit, therefore, must be driven off especially by prayer and psalmody.

LIFE OF SYNCLETICA

First, whenever you undertake to do something good, pray insistently to the Lord that he bring it to completion.

RULE OF BENEDICT

Give yourself frequently to prayer.

RULE OF BENEDICT

Pray for your enemies out of the love of Christ.

RULE OF BENEDICT

Let us ask God in prayer that his will be done in us.

RULE OF BENEDICT

In the winter, from November 1 till Easter, reasonable consideration suggests monks should rise at the eighth hour of the night—that is, so that they can rest until a little after the midpoint of the night, and so rise with digestion completed. Whatever time remains after the night office can be used by those brothers who need to learn the Psalter or the readings. From Easter till November 1, the times shall be arranged that vigils are followed very closely by lauds at daybreak. This provision for a short interval allows the brothers to go out for the needs of nature.

RULE OF BENEDICT

From Holy Easter until Pentecost, Alleluia is sung without exception in both the psalms and the responsories.

RULE OF BENEDICT

Let us therefore render praises to our creator for his just judgments at these times: lauds, prime, terce, sext, none, vespers, compline; and let us rise at night to praise him.

RULE OF BENEDICT

We want to emphasize this: if this arrangement of the psalms displeases anyone, let him arrange them differently if he judges it better.

RULE OF BENEDICT

Those monks who sing less than the Psalter with the customary canticles in the space of a week show themselves indolent in their devout service, since we read that our holy fathers strenuously fulfilled in one day what we lukewarm people take a whole week to complete.

RULE OF BENEDICT

Let us keep in mind how one should act in the sight of God and his angels, and let us so conduct our psalmody that our mind is in tune with our voice.

RULE OF BENEDICT

We should petition the Lord God of all things with all humility and pure devotion.

RULE OF BENEDICT

We should realize that we are heard not by multiplying words, but because of purity of heart and tears of compunction.

RULE OF BENEDICT

Hence, prayer should be brief and pure, unless it happen to be lengthened by an impulse or inspiration of divine grace.

RULE OF BENEDICT

In community [silent] prayer should always be kept short.

RULE OF BENEDICT

Those who wish to pray quietly by themselves at times
when there is no community prayer should simply enter [the
chapel] and pray, not in a loud voice, but in tears and with
full attention of heart.

RULE OF BENEDICT

While the other brothers were asleep, Benedict, the man of
God, was at his vigils, for he had advanced the time of his
night prayers. He was standing at the window praying to
almighty God. Suddenly in the deep of the night he looked
up and saw a light spreading from above. This light drove
back all the darkness of the night. This light shining in the
darkness shone with such brightness that it was brighter
than the day. A very wonderful thing occurred during this
contemplation, for as Benedict himself told afterward, he
saw the whole world as though it had been gathered under a
single ray of the sun. . . . The whole of creation seems narrow to the person gazing at the Creator.

GREGORY THE GREAT, DIALOGUES

Whenever on his travels Wulfstan came to a chapel, neither
haste nor urgent need could move him to pass by without a
visit. He would go in and offer to God and the patron saint
of the church the incense of his prayers with those tears that
someone reported were always ready to flow.

LIFE OF WULFSTAN

When Wulfstan was traveling by horseback, he began the
Psalter as soon as he was mounted on the animal. He didn't
stop until he reached the end. He added litanies with many
collect prayers, as well as vigils and vespers for the souls of
the dead. . . . If he was free of business he always prayed or
preached. If not, with his mind fixed on heaven he longed
for God. When he was lying down, standing, walking,

sitting, there was always a psalm in his mouth and Christ
ever in his heart.

LIFE OF WULFSTAN

In each of his manors, Wulfstan had a little room in which
he shut himself in the morning after mass and locked the
doors. There he found solitude as great as in the desert in
which he meditated on the "contempt of the world" and on
contemplation of God. There was no one to interrupt him
except a cleric who warned him by a knock on the door
that it was time for dinner or the hours.

LIFE OF WULFSTAN

The prayers and meditations that are written down here
were composed in order to arouse the mind of the reader to
love or fear of God or to self-examination. They should not
be read in a rush, but quietly, not cursorily or quickly, but
section by section with intent and leisurely meditation. The
reader should not feel obliged to read any one of them completely, but only to the point that he feels God helping him
to enkindle an impulse to pray, or as much as he likes. Nor is
it necessary that he always begin each one at the beginning;
he can start wherever he wants. The parts are divided up
into paragraphs to make it easier to begin or end at will.
This should prevent the length of the prayers or frequent
repetition from causing boredom; instead, the reader can
gather from them that impulse toward prayer for which they
were composed.

ANSELM OF CANTERBURY, PRAYERS

When you pray, pray in spirit and mind; enter into your
room, close the door, and pray to your father, more with
heart than voice, more with faith than singing.

PETER OF CELLE, THE SCHOOL OF THE CLOISTER

When grace comes first and touches the mind, prayer is en-
joyable and devout. It is like a morning rain shower. Prayer

is laborious when your heart is far away from your prayer, and God is far away from your heart. Your heart is faraway from you if it is preoccupied with unimportant concerns, lukewarm in religious fervor, or immersed in carnal desires. God is away from your heart when he withdraws grace, postpones his presence, or exercises the patience of the petitioner.

PETER OF CELLE, *THE SCHOOL OF THE CLOISTER*

Wordiness in the divine office counts for almost nothing before God.

HILDEGARD OF BINGEN,
EXPLANATION OF THE RULE OF BENEDICT

Now and then, set aside for yourself a day on which, without hindrance, you can be at leisure to praise God and to make amends for all the praise and thanksgiving you have neglected all the days of your life to render to God for all the good he has done. This will be a day of praising and thanksgiving and a day of jubilation, and you will celebrate the memory of that radiant praise with which you will be jubilant to the Lord for eternity, when you will be satisfied fully by the presence of God, and the glory of the Lord will fill your soul.

GERTRUDE THE GREAT, *SPIRITUAL EXERCISES*

Without mental prayer, it would be virtually impossible for frail humanity to bear the fierce struggles of religious life. You can inebriate with sweetness your dryness of heart, making use of the water of prayer drawn from the fountains of the Savior. As a tree experiencing drought sheds its unripened fruit and leaves, so the soul that is deprived of the dew of prayer brings forth incomplete works infected with distaste.

LUDOVICO BARBO, *FORM OF PRAYER*

First, beloved brothers and sisters, you should know that according to the teaching of all the saints who have written

about prayer, there are three ways of praying. The first is
vocal, when one says the Lord's Prayer or a psalm, or reads
some other part of sacred Scripture with devotion, or when
one invokes some devout saint who asks the Lord God for
various graces. . . . This is the common form of prayer,
which is easily understood and is suitable especially for beginners. Great contemplative saints make it their custom to
always start from this form of prayer before ascending to the
other, higher ways of prayer.

LUDOVICO BARBO, *FORM OF PRAYER*

Next, you will ascend to the second stage of prayer—
namely, meditation. When you have been warmed by
vocal prayer, go up to the table of the Lord, to the place
of pasture, to the stage of meditation. Meditation happens
this way: it prays not with words, but in the heart, understanding, and affectivity. For when the works of God and
the order and beauty of creation are represented before the
understanding, the understanding inquires, rejoices, and is
rapt into the love of God, and the affectivity of the soul is
totally suffused with the sweetness in God, moved with love
and zeal in the service and honor of God and the love of
neighbor in God, and attains many other good things at
the same time.

LUDOVICO BARBO, *FORM OF PRAYER*

There is no teaching about the third stage of contemplation,
because ears have not heard nor has it entered into the human heart what things God prepares for the soul, which
God makes ready for divine contemplation. However, I tell
you the truth, beloved brothers: that if you are faithful to the
aforesaid meditations in purity of heart and humility . . .
finally you will arrive at such sweetness, to such love of the
Lord Jesus, that your soul will be totally liquefied as it experiences divine and supertranscendent illuminations.
Your intellect will be faint from stupor since it does not
have the power to examine the depths of this ineffable

enlightenment, whereas your affectivity will be totally en-
flamed and will ascend with elevated heart, tasting God's
beauty.

LUDOVICO BARBO, *FORM OF PRAYER*

We should pray without ceasing because we cannot complete anything without God's help.

JOHN TRITHEMIUS, *RULE*

The divine office is to be prayed by the brethren with the
greatest reverence and faithful intention.

LOUIS DE BLOIS, *MONASTIC STATUTES*

Prayer and meditation have an important part to play in
opening up new ways and new horizons. If our prayer is the
expression of a deep and grace-inspired desire for newness
of life—and not the mere blind attachment to what has
always been familiar and "safe"—God will act in us and
through us to renew the Church by preparing, in prayer,
what we cannot yet imagine or understand. In this way our
prayer and faith today will be oriented toward the future
which we ourselves may never see fully realized on earth.

THOMAS MERTON,
CONTEMPLATION IN A WORLD OF ACTION

Better just to smell a flower in the garden . . . than to have
an unauthentic experience of a much higher value. Better to
honestly enjoy the sunshine or some light reading than to
claim to be in contact with something that one is not in
contact with at all.

THOMAS MERTON,
CONTEMPLATION IN A WORLD OF ACTION

Benedict says that the Lord's Prayer is to be recited aloud
[twice] daily. . . . To fail to forgive is to be trapped in the
past, caught up in resentment and bitterness, staying with
wounds that remain open and raw—everything that will

prevent new life and new growth. It is not only damaging to
the individual, but destructive of community as well. When
I choose not to forgive, I am choosing death rather than life,
and Benedict, who is trying to lead us all the time forward
into freedom and fullness of life, wants to rescue me.

ESTHER DE WAAL, *A LIFE-GIVING WAY*

The opening verse [at most of the hours of the liturgy or
divine office], "God come to my assistance," is a small
phrase commonly used by monastics as a means of recalling
themselves to the presence of God in their mind and heart.
It prompted Cassian to write some of his most inspiring
teaching in which he said that if these words were repeated
throughout the day—at work, in reading, in physical weakness, in moments of temptation—they would lead to a
continuous state of prayer and so to contemplation.

ESTHER DE WAAL, *A LIFE-GIVING WAY*

It is important not to see *lectio divina* as one more technique
or method to be grasped or acquired. It is essentially a
process, and a gentle one. Yet it does have its rhythm and
framework, and it is useful to see this as four steps or rungs.
The first is *lectio* by which we read some short passage from
the Bible. . . . Then comes *meditatio,* which is the seeking,
finding a word or phrase that strikes us, touches us. We repeat it, reflect on it, come to grips with what it is saying to
us personally. . . . The vital thing is that it is to and fro, to
and fro, time and again, until it becomes like a heartbeat inside of [our] own self. For then the word touches the heart
and we reach the third step, *oratio*. . . . It is now that we allow ourselves to be drawn to God as though with a magnet,
and all the false self, with its games and facades, falls away
and instead we surrender totally to God. This brings us to
the final step, *contemplatio,* in which we learn a new language, silence. We are content simply to be, standing in the
presence of God. We let God take us beyond ourselves. . . .
As Abbot Marmion puts it: we read *(lectio)* under the eye of

God *(meditatio)* until the heart is touched *(oratio)* and leaps into flame *(contemplatio)*.

ESTHER DE WAAL, *A LIFE-GIVING WAY*

The function of prayer is not to establish a routine; it is to establish a relationship with God who is in relationship with us always. . . . The function of prayer is to bring us into touch with ourselves, as well. To the ancients, "tears of compunction" were the sign of a soul that knew its limits, faced its sins, accepted its needs and lived in hope.

SR. JOAN CHITTISTER, *THE RULE OF BENEDICT*

"Let the oratory be what it is called," Benedict said. Have a place where you can go in order to be about nothing but the business of being in the presence of God so that every other place in your life can become more conscious of that Presence as well. More than that, Benedict asks us to be there in a special way—with quiet and with awareness, not laughing or talking or lounging or distracting but alert and immersed and enshrouded in the arms of God.

SR. JOAN CHITTISTER, *THE RULE OF BENEDICT*

CHAPTER 2

Reading

The most striking thing about reading in Christian monasticism is that, from the founders of the movement through Benedict to the monastic reformers of the Renaissance, literacy and reading were highly esteemed among monastic theorists, even at times and places when levels of literacy in the surrounding culture were quite low. Such reading was hard work before the invention of printing: the books were often cumbersome, the script difficult to decipher. Perhaps for that reason, but for others that deserve more attention than they have received, monks seem to have regularly failed to read as much as Benedict and Benedictine reformers required of them. They are still failing regularly. In spite of that, the reading of monks—and the production of books that this required—has made a tremendous contribution to Western civilization.

Reading was closely connected with eating; it was food for the soul. As food nourished physical life, reading nourished prayer. Hence, public reading during meals is a very ancient monastic custom. The reading that the members of a community heard in common, at meals and at other times, helped give them their unique culture. Hence, reformers like Louis de Blois urged that on a regular basis members of their congregation listen to certain specific works read out loud. The same realization of the importance of reading in shaping one's mind led monastic teachers to urge that monks not read haphazardly or simply for entertainment. As Saint Benedict said regarding Lenten reading, each monk should be assigned a book and should read it straight through from beginning to end. Many authors urged that important passages be committed to memory and so made one's own in a particularly intimate way.

The primary reading material of the monastic tradition was the Bible. The monks were immersed in a biblical culture, which also defined the flow of the seasons from Advent to Christmas to Lent to Pentecost, to the "little Lent," which began on the Feast of the Holy Cross (September 14). To the Bible were added the works of Christian writers, especially those that commented on the Bible. Beyond that, monks read what background material was necessary for understanding the Bible—everything from grammar books to love poetry.

Medieval readers, monastic and otherwise, were very flexible in their interpretation of texts. In particular, the Bible was thought to have several layers of meaning—literal or historical, doctrinal, and moral—so that readers found moral and spiritual guidance in the strangest places. Each helpful interpretation was thought to be inspired by the Holy Spirit. Hence, the interpretation of texts was a very creative process in which the reader was personally involved.

Jean Mabillon and others warn that unless reading and study are encouraged in the monastery there will not be a suitable pool of educated and intelligent persons from which to choose leaders for the monastic community. It is a monastic commonplace, derived from the *Rule of Benedict* itself, that abbots must teach by word and example. This requires that abbots be well read, both before and after their election.

Mabillon makes a particularly important point when he cautions that at first one should read not to teach others, but simply to form oneself. Later, when one is involved in helping others, one can direct some of one's reading toward their instruction. However, he observes, the latter sort of reading tends not to touch one's own mind and heart so deeply. There also seems to be a law that things read and studied for their own intrinsic worth turn out to be more practical and pastoral than books that aim to offer practical and utilitarian guidance.

Reading habits changed gradually over the centuries. Reading became less devotional, more impersonal. Spiritual reading became distinguished from other sorts of reading: study, recreational reading, informational reading, professional reading, and so forth. It is probably not possible to go back to a steady diet of *lectio divina,* if for no other reason than that reading the Bible today requires the study of technical works of scholarship and commentaries that are not suitable for *lectio divina.* However, monks' reading should continue to be self-reflective and prayerful whenever possible. Just as dedication to prayer should lead to a continuous awareness of the presence of God, so *lectio divina* should lead us to an awareness of God in all the words one reads and hears.

The application of this monastic tradition outside the cloister—and even inside it—becomes steadily more difficult as audio-visual entertainments fill the hours once dedicated to reading. No longer can a monastery assume that its recruits will be regular readers. Perhaps the days of print-based monastic culture are coming to an end. Even if that should be the case, many of the monastic guidelines for reading are applicable to watching videos and television or using the Internet, both in terms of what one should watch and how one should watch it.

Another problem is the growing separation between secular culture and the biblical tradition. Generally, a person who wants to stay current with contemporary culture while at the same time deepening his immersion in the Christian tradition must read two quite separate lists of books. Because contemporary culture is changing so rapidly, there is less time to read the classic and contemporary works of Christian culture, which immerse one in the vision of the church and the rhythms of the liturgy.

This means that religious people, whether in monasteries or out of them, have some difficult choices to make about what and how much to read and watch. The most fundamental choice of all is whether to devote oneself to reading and learning regularly and attentively. The next question is what to read or watch. The monastic tradition would suggest that one should favor the classics, the Bible, and the great writers of the early church, as well as the best biblical scholars, theologians, and creative writers of more recent times. The primary criterion is the formation of the individual in the tradition of which he wants to be a part. Helping others comes next. Impressing them doesn't count for anything.

Something should be said in favor of recreational reading. Eugene

Burke, C.S.P., a distinguished historian of theology, used to tell his classes that he learned the methods of historical research by reading murder mysteries. He might have added that from the best of that genre one can learn style and grace as well. However, the monk or Christian does not need to resort to such half-serious arguments in order to read a murder mystery, a novel, or a book of poetry, or watch a movie or TV program. Reading good literature, which can be described as well-written fiction or poetry that probes the human heart, is a way to connect with the human race, to meet people who think or live differently from us, or to meet people like us coping with the same problems. More than that, literature provides us with a relaxing escape from the pressures of everyday life in a small community. However, too much time devoted to literature or history or thoughtful films, too much time devoted to diversions like murder mysteries or entertaining films, any time devoted to books that prey upon the worst instincts of their readers, is time wasted. Each community and each person has to discern what particular mix of religious and secular reading and viewing is right for them. A criterion of judgment might be whether this reading or viewing helps develop in the person the qualities of character presented in the second part of this book.

[The newly converted Antony] was so attentive at the reading of the Scripture lessons that nothing escaped him: he retained everything and so his memory served him in place of books.

LIFE OF ANTONY

Love to hear holy readings.

RULE OF BENEDICT

The books read at vigils should have divine authority: the Old and New Testaments and explanations of them given by recognized and orthodox catholic fathers.

RULE OF BENEDICT

Reading should never be lacking during meals. Not just anyone who happens to pick up a book should read there. Rather, let the one who is going to read for the whole week begin on Sunday. . . . Let him ask all to pray for him, so that God may divert the spirit of pride from him.

RULE OF BENEDICT

And let there be the deepest silence, so that no one's whispering or voice is heard there except that of the one who is reading.

RULE OF BENEDICT

At all seasons of the year, as soon as supper is over they should all sit together and someone should read the *Conferences* or *Lives of the Fathers* or something else that will edify the hearers, but not the Heptateuch or Kings, because it is not useful for untempered minds to hear these writings at that hour. They ought to be read at other times.

RULE OF BENEDICT

During Lent, they should each receive a book from the library that they are to read straight through to the end.

RULE OF BENEDICT

On Sundays, all should devote themselves to reading, except those who are assigned to special duties.

RULE OF BENEDICT

Let the divine law [i.e., the Bible] be read to guests for their edification.

RULE OF BENEDICT

For someone who is hurrying to the perfection of monastic living, there are the teachings of the holy fathers, whose observance leads one to the heights of perfection. For what page or word of the divine authority of the Old and New Testament is not a carefully honed guideline for human life?

And what book of the holy catholic fathers does not sound the way by which we may reach our creator? And the *Conferences* of the Fathers, their *Institutes* and *Lives,* and the *Rule* of our Father Basil—what else are they but tools of virtues for good and obedient monks?

RULE OF BENEDICT

We have a consoler, our Lord Jesus Christ. Although we cannot see him with bodily eyes, we keep in written form in the Gospels the things he did and taught while he was bodily among us. If we take care to hear, read, and confer with each other about these things, which need to be preserved in our hearts and bodies, we will certainly conquer the obstacles of this age as surely as if the Lord were always standing by us and consoling us.

BEDE, *HOMILIES ON THE GOSPELS*

At Wulfstan's table edifying books were read. Silence was rigorously kept so that all might listen attentively. When the meal was over and the eating place quiet, he would explain what had been read in their native tongue, so that he could provide heavenly alms for those to whom he had already served bodily sustenance.

LIFE OF WULFSTAN

Nicholas was born of distinguished English parents. They had great reverence for the holy man [Wulfstan] and sought in many ways to earn his friendship. Wulfstan baptized Nicholas and saw to it that he was educated. As Nicholas grew up, Wulfstan always had him at his side. In order that learning might be perfected in Nicholas, Wulfstan sent the young man to Kent to be educated under the guidance of Lanfranc. Afterward, in the time of Bishop Thiulf, Nicholas was made prior of Worcester. Within a short time, he had given ample proof of his energy. What I judge to be particularly profitable was that he poured letters and learning into the inhabitants of the place by word and example, so that it

was not exceeded in learning by those great English
churches that are larger than Worcester.

LIFE OF WULFSTAN

When you read, bring a friendly simplicity to the divine law
. . . do not interpret it in novel or erroneous ways. Do not
struggle with questions that do not edify but arouse strife
and the downfall of the listeners. Read to understand; understand to do the commands of God. . . . What lies dead
and deformed in the letter on the dead parchment comes to
life when what is read is put into practice.

PETER OF CELLE,
THE SCHOOL OF THE CLOISTER

Reading is bound to silence. . . . Constant and attentive
reading done devoutly purifies our inner self.

PETER OF CELLE,
THE SCHOOL OF THE CLOISTER

Even if the fruit of understanding and knowledge does not
result from reading, reading is still always useful because
our minds are occupied, and exempted from vain and
useless thinking, which weighs them down and stubbornly
intrudes itself.

PETER OF CELLE,
THE SCHOOL OF THE CLOISTER

Reading should not be vain and garrulous, but quiet and
marked with the seal of meditation.

PETER OF CELLE,
THE SCHOOL OF THE CLOISTER

The Gospel of Matthew . . . begins: "The book of the generation of Jesus Christ" [Mt 1.1]. By this beginning we are
told: "Come and see in this book the mystery hidden from
the ages, revealed and manifest through the generation of

Christ. Come and see the Word incarnate, which has hitherto lain hidden with the Father under the seal of divinity."

PETER OF CELLE,
THE SCHOOL OF THE CLOISTER

I consider a room without reading to be a hell without consolation, an instrument of torture without relief, a prison
without light, a tomb without ventilation, a ditch swarming
with worms, a strangling noose, the empty house of which
the Gospel speaks.

PETER OF CELLE,
ON AFFLICTION AND READING

[Reading] continuously tells of the clash of virtue and
vices. . . . Reading is the food, light, lamp, refuge, solace
of the soul, the spice of all spiritual flavors. It feeds the
hungry, gives light to the one sitting in darkness, offers bread
to the one fleeing shipwreck or war, comforts the contrite
heart.

PETER OF CELLE,
ON AFFLICTION AND READING

Reading seeks a lover to whom she can give not just food,
but offspring; not any sort of lover, but one who is noble,
handsome, thoughtful, healthy, and holy. What is contained
in reading is holy, because holy Scripture contains nothing
that is not holy, since it is inspired by the Holy Spirit.

PETER OF CELLE,
ON AFFLICTION AND READING

[Gertrude] passed beyond the study of the liberal arts and
became a theologian. She pondered untiringly whatever
theological works she had or could obtain and filled the
vault of her heart with the most useful and sweet verses of
holy Scripture. Thus, she always had at hand the divine and
edifying word. Hence, she could always help those who

came to consult her, and she could refute any false idea with scriptural witnesses that were so to the point that no one could argue with her.

GERTRUDE THE GREAT,
THE HERALD OF DIVINE LOVE

She worked tirelessly to collect and transcribe whatever she thought could be useful to others. She did this solely for the honor of God. She was concerned about the salvation of souls, without any thought to human thanks. When people whom she hoped could profit from her writings asked for them, she gave them promptly. If Gertrude discovered that copies of the holy Scriptures were lacking in certain places, she collected as many as she could, in order to gain all for Jesus Christ.

GERTRUDE THE GREAT,
THE HERALD OF DIVINE LOVE

[Gertrude prayed:] May you be glorified if others, in reading these pages, are delighted by the gentleness of your love and are drawn to enjoy in intimacy with you an even greater happiness. Those who study begin by learning the alphabet in order ultimately to arrive at the study of logic. So may these descriptions and these images lead others to taste in themselves this hidden manna, which cannot be known by means of pictures, but for which only those have a hunger who have already tasted it.

GERTRUDE THE GREAT,
THE HERALD OF DIVINE LOVE

[Gertrude concluded:] The more simple readers of this book, who are not strong enough to swim in the river of divine love, can use these pages as a vehicle to help them on the way toward God. May the sight of the graces granted others lead them by the hand, to reading, to meditation, and to contemplation, so that they may begin to taste how sweet is the Lord, and how truly happy is the person who hopes in God and places all his cares in him.

GERTRUDE THE GREAT,
THE HERALD OF DIVINE LOVE

Every interval of time seems short to me, if I am devoting my time to the reading and study of Sacred Scripture. However, if I am not reading or studying, every hour seems tedious and interminable to me. There [in the Bible], I find what I want, I learn what I seek, I am strengthened in hope and taught how to lead my life. There, divine love is announced, the deeds of the saints arouse us to imitate Christ, we develop an avid taste for dwelling in eternal beatitude, and charity enflames the soul.

JOHN TRITHEMIUS, *RULE*

Idle reading corrupts a holy mind.

JOHN TRITHEMIUS, *RULE*

You should listen to the word of God and salutary teaching with a ready and eager mind, no matter who is the speaker. . . . When you want to devote yourself to sacred reading, seek only the honor and glory of God, not idle pleasure or to satisfy vain curiosity or to know many things. In order not to lose your calm and peace of mind by becoming weighed down inside, do not read too much at one time. Read carefully and with an inner desire, not negligently and halfheartedly. Good and salutary things you should always accept as fresh and interesting, even though you have often read or heard them. If you read such things humbly, devoutly, simply, carefully, and reverently, you will derive great utility from them, even if you did not understand them very well. After reading, give thanks to the Lord, and offer to him the things that you have read or heard in eternal praise and in the union of divine love. Ponder these things within yourself, if time is available, and

petition God that you might arrange your life in accord
with them.

LOUIS DE BLOIS, *SPIRITUAL DOCTRINE*

When you properly devote yourself to holy reading, or you
do something else correctly for the praise of God, you often
take away not less but more fruit than if you prayed. For not
only prayers but other salutary words read or heard for the
glory of God, as well as devout actions and thoughts, won-
drously adorn the soul. The mind of a good person receives
from spiritual teaching much that is outstanding and suitable: spiritual teaching preserves from stain, casts out ignorance, makes peaceful, enlightens, nourishes, arouses,
strengthens.

LOUIS DE BLOIS, *SPIRITUAL MIRROR*

Do not imitate those who follow no order in their reading
but are content to read whatever reading chances to come
their way. They are interested in nothing except what is new
and unheard of. Whatever is familiar and everything old,
however useful, bores them. Avoid such instability, for it
does not build up the spirit but scatters it.

LOUIS DE BLOIS, *MIRROR FOR MONKS*

Each day from noon to at least 12:30, if there is no legitimate excuse, a regular public reading should be held in the
chapter room or in the cloister or in some other suitable
place. The readings should include the books of Lawrence
Justinian or the short works of Thomas à Kempis or other
similar devout treatises suitable to monks. When these books
are read through completely, they should be repeated from
the beginning. . . . As regards the readings that are heard
during the community meals, the following plan should
be followed. At the beginning of lunch and dinner, a chapter of the Bible is read. . . . After the reading from holy
Scripture . . . there is added a reading from the holy Doc-

tors, which lasts until the end of the meal. . . . Likewise,
each day before compline there should be reading for about
a quarter of the hour in the chapter room, cloister, or some
other suitable place. . . . At this gathering there should be
readings from the accounts of the martyrs and the lives of
the saints, and the *Conferences* and *Acts* of the Fathers.

LOUIS DE BLOIS, *MONASTIC STATUTES*

While it is true that studies were never the principal purpose
of monks and that they are not necessary for each individual
monk in order for him to reach perfection in his state in
life, one can also say that without studies it is impossible for
monastic communities to maintain order and economy for
a long time.

JEAN MABILLON,
TREATISE ON THE STUDIES OF MONKS

If monasteries cannot last without superiors, one can also
say that in the ordinary course of things there cannot be
good superiors without knowledge. Learning is the superior's guide. . . . That is why all the ancient monastic rules
always put knowledge and wisdom in parallel with goodness of life among the qualities required of an abbot. . . . It
is not sufficient that a superior have acquired knowledge
before undertaking government over his brothers; he must
continue to deepen and augment his knowledge by study
and reading.

JEAN MABILLON,
TREATISE ON THE STUDIES OF MONKS

The spirit in which Scriptures should be read: search first to
know God and the mysteries of our religion, and to know
oneself; and to understand the ways to travel to God, and
how to make good use of creatures. In a word: seek in this
reading only truth and justice and the practice of charity
and the other virtues. The particular qualities needed are

purity of heart, humility, simplicity, control of curiosity, and enthusiasm.

JEAN MABILLON,
TREATISE ON THE STUDIES OF MONKS

If the reading of Scripture is necessary for monks, the reading of the holy Fathers—who are Scripture's true interpreters—is no less important.

JEAN MABILLON,
TREATISE ON THE STUDIES OF MONKS

The two principle goals of monastic studies are knowledge of the truth, and charity or love of justice. . . . It is not only monks who must have these two principal ends in view in their studies, but all Christians. . . . Besides these two principal ends . . . one can also propose some others that are equally advantageous. One of these is to make good use of one's time. . . . In the second place, study can take the place of work, and hence of penance. . . . A third goal of study is to fill one's spirit with holy thoughts and one's heart with devout feelings.

JEAN MABILLON,
TREATISE ON THE STUDIES OF MONKS

In their studies, monks can have the aim of preaching or writing. . . . However, it seems to me dangerous that young religious have this sort of goal in view before they have been filled with truths that they must teach to others. One could say, perhaps, that in working for others, they will fill themselves. But if one considers this more closely, one will see that the things one studies in order to preach or write do not ordinarily enter deeply in the heart of the one studying. . . . I believe therefore that . . . young religious should be occupied in their reading and studies only with care for themselves, that they have in view only to fill their own spirit and heart with the truths they need, and that they leave to Providence and their superiors concerns about applying these truths to others in the future.

JEAN MABILLON,
TREATISE ON THE STUDIES OF MONKS

The contemplative life should liberate and purify the imagination which passively absorbs all kinds of things without our realizing it; liberate and purify it from the influence of so much violence done by the bombardment of social images. . . . The training of the imagination implies a certain freedom and this freedom implies a certain capacity to choose and to find its own appropriate nourishment. Thus in the interior life there should be moments of relaxation, freedom and "browsing." Perhaps the best way to do this is in the midst of nature, but also in literature. Perhaps also a certain amount of art is necessary and music.

THOMAS MERTON,
CONTEMPLATION IN A WORLD OF ACTION

The Rule is totally scriptural. The purpose of the monastic life is to shape life according to the Scriptures. Benedict cites the Bible at every moment.

ESTHER DE WAAL, *A LIFE-GIVING WAY*

The reading of the Word is an essential element of the night office. But Benedict is not content with merely listening to Scripture. He also wants a deepening of our understanding of it. How can we be fed if we do not stretch our minds? It is only too easy to let familiar passages from the Bible drift over me. Benedict wants me to make use of my intellect in my prayer. This means I should study them, use my mind critically, see what others have to say about them, and let myself be humble enough to learn from their interpretation.

ESTHER DE WAAL, *A LIFE-GIVING WAY*

The purpose of reading at meals is a reminder of the whole purpose of the life that Benedict is laying before us: it is so that we should be listening to God at all times. . . . I have been made aware of the attention paid to the needs of the body, but it is no less vital to think of the needs of the mind. It is important to nourish, feed, and enrich the intellect.

ESTHER DE WAAL, *A LIFE-GIVING WAY*

Benedict wants us to do more than read the Scriptures. He wants us to study them, to wrestle with them, to understand them, to make them part of us, to let them grow in us through the work of traditional and contemporary scholarship so that the faith can stay green in us.

SR. JOAN CHITTISTER, *THE RULE OF BENEDICT*

Benedict considers reading such an important part of the meal, in fact, that he insists that the person doing the reading be a good reader, someone who would inspire rather than irritate the souls of the listeners. The reading was to be an artistic event, an instructive experience, a moment of meditation.

SR. JOAN CHITTISTER, *THE RULE OF BENEDICT*

Study is hard work. It is so much easier to find something else to do in its place than to stay at the grind of it. We have excuses aplenty for avoiding the dull, hard, daily attempt to learn. There is always something so much more important to do than reading. There is always some excuse for not stretching our souls with new ideas and insights now or yet or ever.

SR. JOAN CHITTISTER, *THE RULE OF BENEDICT*

CHAPTER 3

Work

The readings in this section are sparse. This may be mere chance, but the small number of quotations does seem to reflect the amount of reflection that monastics have devoted to work. In the realm of monastic theory, work is almost always taken for granted. Saint Benedict insisted that all work was valuable in itself. As Hildegard explains, work engages the monk in God's ongoing work of creation and salvation. Tools deserve the same reverence as chalices and other vessels of the altar. Whether the tool is a shovel or a pen really doesn't make any difference. Both are instruments of good work—of sharing in God's creative activity and of providing for the needs of others.

Monk-workers should be conscientious and reverent; they should use their talents, but be humble about it. Except in dire necessity, they should not be asked to work so much that they are worn out or unhappy. Help should be provided when a task becomes overwhelming. Granted these parameters, monks should work without complaining. Work is natural and necessary. Work is also a way of serving Christ with Christ. Work in which human beings pool their talents and efforts toward a common cause is also a way of uniting us in the Spirit who calls and heals us all.

Benedict and his followers could legislate a benign workload because their primary concerns were neither production nor consumption. If a monastery aimed at sufficiency and no more, the monks would not have to work long hours to produce things to sell or trade. Moreover, monasteries were often the beneficiaries of gifts and donations that helped support the monks and nuns. This enabled them not only to meet their own needs without heroic effort, but also to help others.

Once again one comes back to Benedict's horarium, with its division of the day into prayer, reading, and work. If during the early Middle Ages and often since, prayer has tended to usurp the place of reading and to a lesser degree of work, in recent times it is work that has threatened Benedictine balance. Especially in North American monasticism, work has tended to overshadow all else. The reasons for this are not hard to find. Benedictines came to the United States in the last half of the nineteenth century. They came to serve a immigrant church that was short of personnel and money. Those pioneer monks and sisters generously sacrificed the comforts of the cloister for the challenges of missionary life. They accomplished great feats of evangelization and education. Work was their asceticism. They did not mind working hard, for the tasks were necessary and noble. They established a tradition of hard work that was not without merit. Their intensity and dedication could well serve later generations as examples of how to work hard in the service of others.

In the last half of the twentieth century, when monastics could realistically look to reestablishing a better balance in their lives among work, prayer, and reading, the number of vocations suddenly fell drastically. The population of monasteries became older and older; the number of able-bodied men and women became fewer. In many monasteries it is the heroic efforts of the few that enable the elderly to spend their last years quietly, without fear for the morrow. These able-bodied few are working very hard, and they are very tired.

Unfortunately, the frenetic work schedule of such monastics is matched in our society by the equally inhuman work schedules of many other men and women, especially those with families. For several decades, real income for half or more of the people in our country has risen very little. To compete in the capitalist marketplace, many companies are forcing people to work part-time with partial or no benefits. The new high-tech industries may be glamorous and full of opportunity for the few, but those on the assembly line who are paid eight dollars an hour can support their family only if there are two incomes and minimal expenses. Something similar is happening in universities, where full-time and tenured professors are being replaced with part-time, ill-paid Ph.D.'s who must race from job to job to make a living.

At the other end of the scale, those who hold salaried positions are often expected to work sixty or seventy hours instead of the standard forty. When both spouses work at that pace, family life is minimal at best. All one's best energies go to the job; there is little left for God, for family, for oneself.

In such extreme situations, both monastics and non-monastics have to carve out a life as best they can. One way to take some of the pressure off is to make do with sufficiency rather than abundance or luxury. If this means owning one less car, using the library more, eating simpler, less expensive food and eating at home rather than in restaurants, making fewer trips to the theater, it is perhaps a blessing in disguise. At least necessity and social obligation—to conserve resources, avoid pollution, strengthen the family—will often coincide.

Our pace of work is in part a symptom of very bizarre values. Perhaps if monastics and others could find ways to slow down and work less, they would have time not just for prayer and reading, but also for considering the state of our society and trying to change what is wrong. When one ponders a society where people are tempted to spend most of their waking hours in frantic work or mindless television viewing, ordering time to make a place not just for work, but for reading, reflection, and prayer—and some social activism—seems eminently rational.

An old man said: "Never have I desired a work that was useful to me but that caused harm to my brother, for I have this firm hope: that my brother's advantage is for me a work full of fruit."

SAYINGS OF THE DESERT FATHERS AND MOTHERS

In whatever work that you do, you should say to yourself at every moment: "If God looks at me, what does he see?"
Then see how you answer yourself. If you condemn yourself, leave immediately. Stop the work that you were doing

and take up something else in order to be sure to reach your destination. For it is necessary that the traveler be always ready to continue his journey. When you are seated at manual labor, when you are walking along the road, when you are eating, tell yourself this: "If God called me now, what would happen?" See how your conscience answers and hurry to do what it tells you.

SAYINGS OF THE DESERT FATHERS AND MOTHERS

If you are at your manual labor in your room and it comes time to pray, do not say: "I will use up my supply of branches or finish weaving the little basket, and then I will rise," but rise immediately and render to God the prayer that is owed him. Otherwise, little by little you come to neglect you prayer and your duty habitually, and your soul will become a wasteland devoid of every spiritual and bodily work. For right at the beginning your will is apparent.

SAYINGS OF THE DESERT FATHERS AND MOTHERS

A monk was working on the feast day of a martyr. Another monk saw him and asked: "Are we allowed to work today?" The other answered: "On this day the servant of God was tortured and died a martyr. And should I not tire myself a bit by working?"

SAYINGS OF THE DESERT FATHERS AND MOTHERS

The old men said of one of the brothers that he never stopped his manual labor but his prayer ascended continually before God. He was very humble and very stable.

SAYINGS OF THE DESERT FATHERS AND MOTHERS

The brothers should serve one another.

RULE OF BENEDICT

Let all have help according to the size of the community and the circumstances of the place.

RULE OF BENEDICT

If the community is large, the cellarer [business manager, in charge of material goods] should receive helpers to assist him so he can fulfill the office committed to him with an untroubled mind. Requests should be made and supplies handed out at the proper hours so that no one will be disturbed or unhappy in the house of God.

RULE OF BENEDICT

An hour before mealtime, the weekly servers should receive an extra portion of bread and drink over and above the regular allotment, so that then they may serve the rest of the community at mealtimes without murmuring or heavy fatigue.

RULE OF BENEDICT

At the end of Sunday lauds, those beginning or completing a week of table service should bow down in the oratory before all the community and ask them to pray for them.

RULE OF BENEDICT

This principle pertains to all tasks in the monastery: when they need help, let it be given them, and when they have nothing to do, they should do what they are told.

RULE OF BENEDICT

The house of God should be wisely managed by wise people.

RULE OF BENEDICT

If there are artisans in the monastery, let them work at their arts with all humility.

RULE OF BENEDICT

If some of the work of the artisans is to be sold, let those who conduct the sale make sure there is no fraud. . . . They should make sure that the vice of avarice does not affect the prices. Let things always be sold somewhat more cheaply than they can be by secular people, so that in all things God may be glorified.

RULE OF BENEDICT

Let them direct to God the works that they do, because human work that is directed to God will shine in the heavens. . . . For God created human beings and placed other creatures under them so that they might act on other creatures in such a way that God's good works would not be destroyed.

HILDEGARD OF BINGEN, *BOOK OF LIFE'S MERITS*

When someone, through the gift of the Holy Spirit, rightly and properly imposes on himself labors to meet some need of the living or for the repose of the dead, God receives his toil as right and just, just as he heard Moses and Eli when they worked ceaselessly on behalf of those who had sinned against God. . . . Therefore, every believer should never stop working for God, on behalf of others as well as himself, because God will look into the hearts of men and reward their just labor and goodwill.

HILDEGARD OF BINGEN, *BOOK OF LIFE'S MERITS*

Just as the work of God, which mankind is, will not be exterminated, but will rather endure, so also human work will not fade away, because human work that is directed toward God will shine in the heavens. . . . When God created human beings, he enjoined them to work on created things. And just as he will not come to an end—he will be changed into ashes but afterward he will rise—so his good works will be seen unto glory.

HILDEGARD OF BINGEN, *BOOK OF LIFE'S MERITS*

When the excellence of God is praised by human beings, it is as if honor were shown to God by the earth itself in the just and holy works of human beings who arise from that earth. . . . Human beings, who are animated by the power of reason and the spirit of intelligence, are made from the earth. The material of God's work is in them who are the material of the humanity of the Son of God, because that handiwork which God made into human beings from the earth was also the material of that Virgin who brought forth the Son of God without any blemish in his pure and holy humanity. . . . The soul is the matter of good works and of a better life, which is a divine element in the powers of the soul, for it is from God and exists in human beings who prepare for just and well-ordered works in response to the divine command and then begin to do them; then the incarnate Son of God completes them in the perfection of his blessed virtues and in manifesting true holiness. Thus existent life gives life to those who believe in it.

HILDEGARD OF BINGEN, *BOOK OF LIFE'S MERITS*

Benedict's idea seems to be that the monk gives glory to God precisely by not working as others do, for material gain or for popular success. This can easily escalate and become competitive, in a search for more money, a better reputation.

ESTHER DE WAAL, *A LIFE-GIVING WAY*

Work done in the Benedictine tradition is supposed to be regular; it is supposed to be productive, it is supposed to be worthwhile, but it is not supposed to be impossible.

SR. JOAN CHITTISTER, *THE RULE OF BENEDICT*

CHAPTER 4

Mutual Support

Human relationships in a monastery are not quite the same as those in any other setting. Monastics take vows that bind them to their community for life. In this there is some analogy to marriage vows. A monastery is like a family, but it is not a family. The ties between monks are not ties of kinship. Nor are they for the most part ties of close friendship. Monastics are sometimes friends with each other, but a monk is more likely to have friends outside his cloister than inside it. This is mostly because of numbers: if a friend is one in a thousand, the chances of finding a close friend in a monastery are not very high. The closest analogue to the ties that bind a monastic community together is probably found among longtime neighbors, who get along with each other, who trust and can count on each other—people bound to each other by seldom examined but time-tested and sturdy ties.

The most important relationship in the monastery is that of the monk to God. Upon that relationship depends all the others. The bedrock of one's relation to God is faith: a firm conviction that God is there for each of us and all of us together. For the Christian and the Christian monk, this faith centers on Christ. For the *Rule of Benedict* Christ is the divine Son of God and Lord of Life and the sick person with special needs, the inconvenient guest, and each monk. So, ultimately, the relationship of monk to monk is the relationship of monk to Christ and, indeed, Christ to Christ.

In spite of the uniqueness and deeply Christian basis of the relationships in a monastery, monks have much to teach about how people can get along together in families, communities, and places of work. The Benedictine emphasis on community is rooted in a long-standing monastic conviction that if a person is not properly related to her neighbors, that person is not properly related to Christ. There is a provision in the *Rule of Benedict* for monks to go from the community to live a solitary life at a distance from the community. Such solitary life takes many forms, but it is universally agreed that leaving the community for a solitary life ought not be an escape from the need to relate to others or a way to avoid facing the selfishness and narcissism and fear and impatience that make others unbearable, that make well-meaning, flawed human beings seem like enemies.

Saint Antony said: "From our neighbor comes life or death." To prevent the possibility of death coming in this way, Benedict provided that every day, morning and evening, the abbot should lead the community in the Lord's Prayer, because in that prayer monks declare, "Forgive us our offenses as we forgive those who offend us." Equally important is Benedict's admonition that the sun should not go down on one's anger. He even provides somewhat ritualized procedures for dealing with anger and alienation. Medieval monasteries had some interesting ways of dealing with hostilities, including a daily meeting in which there was a ritualized opportunity to accuse oneself or others of faults against the peace and order of the community. Monasteries today are experimenting with new models of dealing with anger, irritation, and misunderstanding. Sometimes they have a counselor or psychological consultant help them. The goal, of course, is to have a community of honest and tolerant adults.

One of the key elements in living peacefully together is to avoid judging others. One can spend an entire vespers surveying the monks—evaluating their singing, their posture, their enunciation—then move to dinner and evaluate their table manners. Whatever criterion one uses, it will usually be one on which one scores very highly oneself. People who naturally wear old, cheap clothes mercilessly judge those who wear fancy clothes for their extravagance. People who dress nicely mercilessly judge those who wear inexpensive clothes for their sloppiness and embarrassing lack of style.

Hostility, unchecked, grows into sullen avoidance, silence, or, worse, retaliation. Several monasteries have stories about monks who liked to park their power mowers outside the room or classroom of a fellow monk to irritate him and thus gain revenge for some real or imagined slight. The next step is to gossip and criticize, to complain to people who share one's point of view and so divide the community into opposing camps.

All these sins against community are mentioned in the readings. For those who would like still more analysis of the psychological underlay of human conflict in community, there is the ruthless analysis in Saint Bernard's treatise *On the Stages of Humility and Pride.*

"From our neighbor comes life or death." Enough has been said of death; what about life? The monastic tradition makes much of the notion of mutual service. Where feasible, monks serve each other in the dining room, taking turns at cooking, serving, and doing the dishes. If that is not possible, they at least divide up cleaning tasks among themselves. In this way all the monks serve, and they work together, which can help cement the bonds that connect them.

Beyond such mutual service, there are the needs that arise unexpectedly. Someone suddenly has too much to do, or someone becomes ill. At that point, the monastic tradition says the rest of the community should be willing and able to help. Willing, because of the mutual commitment that binds the community together, and able, because people's schedules are not so inflexible and full that they cannot find time to help a brother, or sister, wife, or child, in need.

To share one's talents with the community and to value the talents of others as though they were one's own was perhaps easier in ages in which there was a stronger sense of community. Yet even today there seems to be no basis, other than our essential interconnectedness, upon which envy and selfishness can be eliminated, and scope given for each person's talents to unfold and contribute to the good of all.

> Antony said, "From our neighbor comes life or death. If we win over our brother, we have gained God, but if we scandalize our brother, we have sinned against Christ."
>
> ANTONY, *SAYINGS*

Some brothers came to the Abba Antony and said to him,
"Speak a word that tells us how are we to be saved." The old
man said to them, "You have heard the Scriptures. That
should be enough for you." But they said, "We want to hear
from you too, Father." Then the old man said to them, "The
Gospel says, if anyone strikes you on the right cheek, turn to
him the other also" [Mt 5.39]. They said, "We cannot do
that." The old man replied, "If you cannot turn the other
cheek, at least allow one cheek to be struck." "We cannot do
that either," they said. So he said, "If you are cannot even
do that, do not return evil for evil." Once more they said,
"We cannot do that either." Then the old man said to his
disciple, "Prepare a little brew of corn for these invalids."
Then he said to the brothers: "If you cannot do this, or that,
what can I do for you? What you need is prayers."

ANTONY, SAYINGS

[The evil spirits] envy us at all times. [They corrupt our relations with each other in three noteworthy ways:] the judgments which they sow in our hearts, causing us, when we
are sitting alone, to judge the brothers who are not with us;
the contempt they set in our hearts by pride when we are
hard-hearted and despise each other, when we are bitter
against each other with our hard words, grieving at every
hour, accusing each other and not ourselves, thinking that
our struggle is from our fellows, passing judgment on what
appears outwardly, while the robbers are all inside our
house; and the disputes and divisions we have with each
other until we establish our own words to appear justified
in the face of each other.

ANTONY, LETTERS

[The demons] know that our destruction is from our neighbor, and our life is also from our neighbor.

ANTONY, LETTERS

Whoever sins against his neighbor sins against himself.

ANTONY, *LETTERS*

Whoever knows himself knows all human beings. . . . But whoever can love himself loves all human beings.

ANTONY, *LETTERS*

And likewise if someone, being human, is found blameworthy, we do not judge him. God is the judge, and in each case he has, as judges under himself, the successors of the Apostles, able in Spirit to "judge according to what is right" [Jn 7.24]. As for us among the flock, we must be compassionate and merciful to each other.

LIFE OF PACHOMIUS

For what is greater than such a vision, to see the invisible God in a visible human being, his temple?

LIFE OF PACHOMIUS

One day Abba Pachomius himself told the brothers about this, which is a kind of vision: "I once saw a large place with many pillars in it. And there were in the place many men unable to see where to go, some of them going around the pillars, thinking they had traveled a long distance toward the light. And a voice [resounded] from all directions: 'Behold! Here is the light!' They would turn back to find it, only to hear the voice again and turn back another time. There was great wretchedness. Afterwards I saw a lamp moving, followed by many men. Four of them saw it and the others followed them, each holding his neighbor's shoulder lest he go astray in the dark. And if anyone let go of the man in front of him, he would go astray with those following him. Recognizing two of them who had let go of their neighbor, I shouted to them, 'Hold on, lest you lose yourselves and the others.' And guided by the lamp, those who followed it came up to this light through an opening."

He told these things to some brothers in private. And
we heard it from them much later, along with the following
interpretation: "This world is the dark [place, which is dark]
because of error, each heretic thinking to have the right
path. The lamp is the faith of Christ, which saves those who
believe aright and leads to the kingdom of God."

LIFE OF PACHOMIUS

It is essential, then, to be on guard against remembrance of
wrongs, for many terrible consequences develop from it:
envy, sadness, malicious talk. The evil of these vices is lethal,
even if they seem to occur in small doses.

LIFE OF SYNCLETICA

[Those] courageous in disposition and strong in will, live
with the weak and share their lives in their desire to save
them. And, to be sure, they are censured by people on the
outside and mocked by those who see them spending their
lives with people less disciplined. [Their behavior] is like the
Lord's for the Lord ate with tax collectors and sinners. Their
attitude is characterized by brotherly love rather than self-
love for they regard those who sin as houses on fire; giving
no thought to their own interests, they apply their efforts to
save what belongs to others. . . . Good people have placed
their own possessions second to the salvation of others. This
is the sign of genuine love. These people are the custodians
of pure love.

LIFE OF SYNCLETICA

Give aid to the poor, clothe the naked, visit the sick, bury
the dead, help those in difficulty, console the sorrowing.

RULE OF BENEDICT

Above all, the cellarer should have humility, and when he
has no material goods to give someone who asks, he should
at least offer a kind reply.

RULE OF BENEDICT

Let them serve one another, and let none be excused from kitchen duty, unless they are sick or occupied with some important business, because from such service a greater reward and charity are acquired. . . . Helpers should be provided for those who are weak so that they will not find their work depressing. In fact, let all have help according to the size of the community and the nature of the place. The rest should serve one another in love.

RULE OF BENEDICT

Before and above all else, care is to be given to the sick, for Christ is really served in them. . . . But let the sick keep in mind that they are served for the honor of God and not distress those who are serving them by their excessive demands.

RULE OF BENEDICT

The weakness of the elderly and of children should be kept in mind, and the rule should not be strictly applied to them in regard to food. Rather, let them be treated with loving consideration.

RULE OF BENEDICT

Special care is to be taken that on no occasion anyone presume to defend another in the monastery or, at it were, to take another under his protection.

RULE OF BENEDICT

Love your enemies.

RULE OF BENEDICT

Let them vie in giving one another honor. Let them patiently bear everyone's weaknesses of body and behavior. Let them compete in obeying one another. Let no one do what he judges beneficial to himself, but what is better for another. Let them practice chaste love in the community. Let them fear God out of love. Let them love their abbot with a sincere and humble love. Let them prefer nothing to Christ. May Christ lead us together to eternal life.

RULE OF BENEDICT

What can I, a beggar and a pauper, a worm and ashes, what can I return to my God, if not that I keep his command with all my heart? It is your command that we love one another.

ANSELM OF CANTERBURY,
PRAYERS AND MEDITATIONS

[Gertrude] was wont to say that as long as she kept them for herself and her own enjoyment, all the things that she, unworthy and ungrateful, received unmerited from the overflowing goodness of the Lord seemed to her like treasures hidden in muck. However, if she shared them with a neighbor, these favors became like a precious stone set in pure gold.

GERTRUDE THE GREAT,
THE HERALD OF DIVINE LOVE

Do not look on others with too severe a countenance, nor let your mind be stern and bitter. Instead, be transformed by kindly feelings, and show yourself to have a gentle, benevolent, affable, and ready heart toward everyone. But if anger or indignation should suddenly move or provoke you, or you feel bitterness toward anyone, take care not to give in to this wicked impulse, but reprove, soften, and extinguish it as much as you can. Regret that your heart is still so bitter. Humble yourself and ask God's help. Once he has bountifully poured the sweetness of charity into you, you will no longer be bitter. Often God allows his chosen friends to be prone to anger, so that they may know themselves more deeply and stand fast more firmly in humility.

BLOSIUS, *SPIRITUAL MIRROR*

Be there with a ready will for those who need your help.

BLOSIUS, *SPIRITUAL MIRROR*

[Monastic community] has been from the beginning, a grace of communion in shared quest and a participated light. It is then a charism of special love and of mutual aid in the attainment of a difficult end, in the living of a hazardous and austere life. . . . Monastic work, obedience, poverty, chastity, are all in some way colored and tempered by the communal charism of brotherhood in pilgrimage and in hope.

THOMAS MERTON,
CONTEMPLATION IN A WORLD OF ACTION

One is not absolutely alone, . . . one cannot live and die for himself alone. My life and my death are not purely and simply my own business. I live by and for others, and my death involves others.

THOMAS MERTON,
CONJECTURES OF A GUILTY BYSTANDER

How glad I am to find this short chapter on the celebration of Vigils or Matins on the anniversaries of the saints. It adds another dimension to the sense of time and order that Benedict is giving us. . . . I am inserted into a community here on earth; I am also part of a community in the wider context of the Church beyond time and space. It makes me think in gratitude of what I owe to the saints, living and dead, known and unknown.

ESTHER DE WAAL, *A LIFE-GIVING WAY*

There is to be acceptance of people who come from very different places (using this metaphorically as well as literally). There is to be willingness to hear "reasonable criticisms or observations" and to learn from the example of others. . . . In a world that builds barriers, puts up walls, keeps the other out, and is looking for certainty, we turn to the Rule and find a man who insists on balance, mutual re-spect, reciprocity, openness. [Benedict] . . . refused to live with a closed mind.

ESTHER DE WAAL, *A LIFE-GIVING WAY*

Complaining is the acid that shrivels our own souls and the soul of the community around us as well.

SR. JOAN CHITTISTER, *THE RULE OF BENEDICT*

CHAPTER 5

Hospitality

A month ago a missionary priest from Mexico, on sabbatical from teaching in a seminary, asked if he could stay at our monastery for four or five weeks. The community gladly said yes. Today I received a letter from a longtime friend, who wrote that her son may write to ask if he can stay at our monastery for a while. He is searching and finds life somewhat mystifying. He would like a place of retreat where he could strive for perspective and a plan. If he writes, I hope we invite him to spend some time with us. Today such requests to monasteries are not uncommon, but they are hard to honor. There are so many factors: groups wanting to rent the guest house, guests who might be frightened by the presence of a stranger none of us knows, the costs of room and board, possible legal liability.

The situation in early monasticism was quite different. In a harsh desert environment, where hospitality was a much simpler issue, a matter of life or death, monks never hesitated to be hospitable. In such places people don't lock the doors to the storerooms when they leave home, and they welcome whoever comes. The desert fathers taught that monks should interrupt their prayers and break their fasts in order to welcome guests. Even when monasteries appeared in fertile lands and cities, they maintained this tradition of hospitality.

Benedict and the tradition after him struggled with treating all people fairly. Noble guests and bishops received one sort of hospitality, paupers and pilgrims another. Yet everyone knew that if Christ came to visit, he would be found among the paupers. So the ideal remained: treat all as though they were Christ.

Today, the great enemies of any such universal hospitality are busyness, fear, and professionalism. If I don't have time to talk to the person calling for help, hospitality is out of the question. The advent of a guest, like the unanticipated needs of fellow monks, is a gauge of our use of time. If we have no time for the guest, our day is too full. However, busyness can be an independent sin against the stranger, or it can be an excuse concocted because we don't want to say we are afraid or prefer to remain uninvolved.

We are afraid of violence and sexual assault, of robbery and vandalism. We want to avoid aggressive intrusions into our business and our privacy by salesmen and poll takers. Violence and intrusion are genuine dangers, but perhaps we have too much to lose, too many things clung to so tightly that the possibility of losing them looms too large. Professionalism becomes a problem when, rather than welcome needy strangers, I immediately think how to shunt them to the appropriate agency, get them a voucher from the food bank, or send them to the downtown mission.

Positively, hospitable people have more fun. They meet Christ in the strangest guises. Several years ago I was spending Lent at a mission in the high desert about five miles from a town of one hundred people. The enterprises of the town closed up on Sundays. Two vans of people drove up and knocked on my door. They were looking for a bathroom. There was none in the town and no trees in the desert. My little church and trailer looked semiofficial, so to me they came as their last hope. A string of fourteen people snaked from the inside of the trailer and out onto the porch. Nobody talked or made any fast moves until after they had reached the head of the line. Then we visited a bit, but I couldn't convince any of them to have some juice or a soft drink.

Observers tell us that contemporary American society needs to strengthen the communities that are intermediate between the government on the one hand and the family on the other: neighborhood, clubs, service organizations, parishes, and all the sorts of voluntary organizations. It is said that if each church in America would sponsor one family's housing, all involuntary homelessness would be eliminated. If neighbors could be hospitable to each other's children, some of the difficulties latchkey children experience would be solved.

Hospitality requires discipline on the part of the host. The host provides a place where the guest or stranger is secure and respected. The host may provide options, but it is not the host's task to fill up all the guest's time with activities or her space with noise or things. The good host has no ambition to control the space made available to strangers or to control the strangers themselves.

Presupposing the proper management of time, requiring that we overcome some of our fears and our need to control and that we invite people as equals and indeed as Christ, hospitality is an art and a school requiring the exercise of most of the qualities of character valued in the Benedictine tradition and discussed in the rest of this book.

A brother came to visit a hermit. As he was taking his leave, he said: "Pardon me, father, for I have caused you to violate your rule." But the hermit answered: "My rule is to refresh you and send you back in peace."

SAYINGS OF THE DESERT FATHERS AND MOTHERS

A hermit lived near a monastery. He lived a very austere life. Now it happened that some visitors came to the monastery and caused him to eat outside of the usual mealtime. After that, the brothers said to him: "Father, were you not distressed?" He said to them: "My distress is to do my own will."

SAYINGS OF THE DESERT FATHERS AND MOTHERS

There was talk of an old man who dwelt in Syria near a desert road. This was his task: whenever a monk came from the desert, he cheerfully provided him with refreshment. One day there came a hermit for whom he wished to provided refreshment. However, the other did not wish to accept anything, saying that he was fasting. The old man was saddened and said to him: "Do not neglect your servant, I pray you, nor despise me: let us pray together. See this tree

here? We will yield to whichever of us causes it to bow
when he places his knee to the ground and prays." The hermit knelt then in order to pray, and nothing happened. Then
the hospitable monk knelt and the tree bent over with him.
Reassured in this way, they gave thanks to God.

SAYINGS OF THE DESERT FATHERS AND MOTHERS

Two brothers came one day to see an old man. Now the old
man had the custom of eating only every other day. When
he saw the brothers, he rejoiced and said: "Fasting brings its
recompense; but whoever eats because of charity fulfills two
precepts: he abandons his own will, and he fulfills the law of
charity." And he gave refreshment to the brothers.

SAYINGS OF THE DESERT FATHERS AND MOTHERS

All guests who arrive should be received as Christ. . . .
When guests are announced, let them be met by the superior or some members of the community with every mark
of love. Let them first pray together, and so socialize in
peace. . . . All arriving or departing guests should be greeted
with profound humility. . . . One must adore Christ in
them, for he is in fact the one who is received.

RULE OF BENEDICT

Let all kindness be shown to guests. The superior should
break his fast for the guest unless it is a special fast day that
must be observed. . . . Let the abbot wash the hands of the
guests; the feet of all guests should be washed by both the
abbot and the community.

RULE OF BENEDICT

The greatest care is to be shown in the reception of the
poor and of pilgrims, because in them especially, Christ is
received; fear of the rich demands that the wealthy be
treated with respect.

RULE OF BENEDICT

[Wulfstan's hospitality to some high-ranking visitors from
Rome] left nothing undone, so that they would know the
bounteous hospitality of the English. . . . Every day
Wulfstan took care of three poor people. At the Lord's
command he gave them their daily bread and washed
their feet.

LIFE OF WULFSTAN

O God, you visit the humble and you console us with mutual love. Stretch forth your grace to our community so that
we may become aware of your coming into our midst
through those in whom you dwell.

WULFSTAN OF WORCESTER, *PORTIFOLIUM*

For it is as though Christ is present when guests arrive and
they receive them, or when guests depart and they bless
them as they go, or they bow before the guests out of reverence for Christ or ask pardon from them. Benedict adds immediately: "And after this let all courtesy be shown him."

HILDEGARD OF BINGEN,
EXPLANATION OF THE RULE OF BENEDICT

When upright men and friends arrive, [the monks] can
speak with them at suitable times about whatever is proper,
even if it is outside the time for community conversation.

LOUIS DE BLOIS, *MONASTIC STATUTES*

What does it mean to receive another as Christ? I find
that the story of Benedict at Subiaco, which St. Gregory
records in the *Dialogues,* gives me an illuminating glimpse.
Benedict has been alone in the cave for three years, in silence and in solitude, when he is visited by a priest—sent
specially by God, who wished Benedict to have company at
Easter. The scene is charming and really very humorous.
Benedict is so deep in prayer and so far away from everything that he has no idea that it is Easter, but to the priest's

greeting he replies: "Easter it is indeed since I have the joy of seeing you." In the face of the first person that he sees, Benedict finds the first fruits of the resurrection and of the new world to which he is called.

ESTHER DE WAAL, *A LIFE-GIVING WAY*

We cannot be too busy, too professional, too removed from the world of the poor to receive the poor and sustain the poor. . . . To practice hospitality in our world, it may be necessary to evaluate all the laws and all the promotions and all the invitation lists of corporate and political society from the point of view of the people who never make the lists. Then hospitality may demand that we work to change things.

SR. JOAN CHITTISTER, *THE RULE OF BENEDICT*

PART TWO

Character

Having looked at the five activities into which the Benedictine tradition divides the monk's day, we turn now to the sort of person that tradition thought a monk should be. A monk was to have certain qualities of character that guided the way he carried out those five activities and were honed and strengthened in the process.

I am not the first person in Benedictine history to draw up a list of desirable traits. Speaking in one of his homilies about the workings of the Holy Spirit, Bede distinguished virtues that are stable character traits, and unusual gifts that come and go. Bede's list has a monastic ring to it:

> Note that the Holy Spirit always remained in the Lord, but in holy men and women, while they still bear their mortal bodies, the Spirit partly remains and partly leaves, perhaps to return again later. The Spirit remains within them so that they may be zealous for good deeds, love voluntary poverty, seek gentleness, mourn with desire for the eternal, hunger and thirst for justice, embrace mercy, purity of heart, and the tranquillity of peace, and also so that they may not be afraid to suffer persecution for the sake of acting justly and they may desire to dedicate themselves to alms, prayers, fasting, and the rest of the fruits of the Spirit. He withdraws for a time so that they do not always have the ability to cure the sick, raise the dead, cast out demons, or even prophesy. The Spirit always remains so that they can have virtue and live wondrously. The Spirit comes intermittently so that they can manifest to others through miraculous signs what they are within.

Saint Gertrude wrote in her *Spiritual Exercises:*

Dear Jesus, . . .
make me perfect in fearing you.
Make me pleasing to you
in humility of spirit,
in sisterly charity,
in chaste simplicity,
in humble modesty,
in purity of heart,
in the guarding of my senses,
in holiness of life,
in ready obedience,
in gentle patience,
in spiritual discipline,
in freely chosen poverty,
in holy leniency,
in maturity of conduct,
in cheerfulness of spirit, and
in all truth,
in good conscience,
in steadfast faith,
in holy perseverance,
in strength of hope,
in fullness of charity, and
in the blessed consummation of your cherishing-love:
so that the thornbush of my heart may be converted
into a paradise of all virtues and a red berry bush of total
perfection, as if it were a field blessed by the Lord, full
of all peace, holiness, and devotion.

Peter of Celle was fond of such lists also, although he listed components of cloistered life and not simply virtues. A composite of five of his lists in *The School of the Cloister* includes the following: simplicity and frugality in food, drink, clothing, sleep, and speech; external conduct that is humble and acceptable to outsiders; seclusion; fraternal love and obedience to superiors; fear and awareness of death and hell; fear, obedience, and love of God; confession and sorrow for sins; prayer in choir and in private; reading; and perseverance.

Thomas Merton, who agonized over the definition of monastic life and the role of the writer within it, also developed a list in the text of some conferences, printed in *Contemplation in a World of Action:* separation from ordinary life outside the cloister; charismatic freedom; asceticism (the price of freedom); the discipline of listening to God; community; prayer; and penance.

In the end, we are judged by who we have become rather than what we have accomplished. When we are young we may think that doing is more important than being, but time disabuses us of this notion. Most of us find we can accomplish much less than we'd hoped. More important, we discover to our horror that what we do is colored by who we are. Our every vice and defect tends to leave a smudge on the things we do and build and on the people we influence.

Benedict is almost entirely indifferent to material results. He doesn't ask whether the cellarer makes the monastery rich; he asks how the cellarer treats the monks. He does not ask if the abbot is popular, but whether he has helped his monks grow as sons of God and human beings. Monastic success is a matter of people-making for God, not of numbers or affluence or even influence. The monastery is a school of virtue or good habits and a school of divine service. In the end, virtue and divine service coalesce. For the glory of God, said Irenaeus, an early Christian writer, is a human being who is fully alive.

The school of virtue is the community in which one finds oneself. We are life or death for each other. From others we learn honesty. Their presence invites us to live for something greater than ourselves. They are, in fact, the abiding sacrament of Christ. So I must listen humbly to what they say, to what God tells me through them, and then put their message into practice. When life with these others—abbot and fellow monks in the monastery; wife, husband, parent, children, friends, neighbors, and colleagues elsewhere—becomes unbearable, then I will learn patience and the hard lessons of peace. Somehow, with and through them, I will find the strength to resist the lure of an indulgent, consumerist society that is confused about what makes people whole and happy.

Virtue does not give us easy answers or certainty. Virtue hones our skills so that in each situation we can listen carefully to our hearts, to the advice or commands of others, to the still whisper of God, and then act with discretion. Discretion, we shall see, is the pivotal monastic virtue. Rooted in self-knowledge and attentiveness, discretion guides us in each situation. There are rules and they are necessary, but they are secondary. Listening and wise choices are primary. Mozart couldn't have composed without staffs, and scales and tempo, but his genius was in how he composed something unique and beautiful within that framework. Each of us is called to compose a unique and beautiful person, with the rules of morality and the circumstances of our lives to provide parameters and the voice of God and the advice of others to inspire us.

[The Virtues declare:] The Word of God grew bright in human form, and therefore we shine with him, building up the members of his beautiful body.

HILDEGARD OF BINGEN, *ORDO VIRTUTUM*

The one who has set his foot on the way of the virtues lives more securely in the cloister than out of it, for as the proverb says: "Woe to those who are alone; when they fall, they have no one to help them up" [Eccl 4.9].

JOHN TRITHEMIUS, *RULE*

To attain the promises of God, we need above all continuous exercise in the virtues; for however firm one's commitment to some good may be, if it is not renewed daily, it quickly dies out.

JOHN TRITHEMIUS, *RULE*

This school of virtue—the monastic life!

JOHN TRITHEMIUS, *RULE*

This is the school of virtues, in which the reader-instructor is Christ, the book is conscience, and the rod is the fear of the Lord.

JOHN TRITHEMIUS, *RULE*

Benedict does not give me certainty. He does not give me easy answers. He gives me a focus, shows me the stance. He is forming me so that I can respond to each new situation, each new demand. He knows about the weakness and frailty of human nature and how we tend to cling when we are frightened and insecure. That sort of dependency is disastrous. Benedict has such a respect for each one of us that he pays us this compliment of refusing to stifle our freedom.

ESTHER DE WAAL, *A LIFE-GIVING WAY*

CHAPTER 6

Silence and Speech

Silence and speech are the two forms of communication that cement community. Writing for their fellow monks but with suggestions that could find a place in any human community from family to parish, Thomas Merton speaks of true and false communication and Jean Mabillon searches for ways in which speech could be formed into an instrument for sharing information.

The first word in the *Rule of Benedict* is "Listen!" Monastic life is a training in the art of listening, which begins in silence, develops in attentiveness, and is perfected in communication. The first seven chapters of Benedict's *Rule* are devoted to fundamental topics. Chapter 5 is on obedience (a form of active listening); and chapter 6 is on reticence. In chapter 4, Benedict urges monks to avoid much talking, evil or silly talk, and raucous laughter. These admonitions are repeated in chapter 7 regarding humility, which is itself a prerequisite for effective listening and communication.

Silence is a dwindling resource in the contemporary world. Rock music blasts at the onlookers at NBA games, country music played over loudspeakers entertains patrons at self-service gas stations, the insipid music in elevators and on phone answering systems is presumably designed to soothe those who find waiting an aggravation. Meanwhile, sirens provide an overlay of random noise that sounds above the ordinary buzzes and bangs and squeaks of daily life.

Silence is usually the first impression of visitors to a monastery. Such silence is not necessarily emptiness, a mere background to sound. Silence can be full and alert, or a static-free medium of communication.

The principal enemy of interior and exterior silence for most of us is our own tongue. Perhaps we fear the emptiness within us and take refuge in speech. Speech serving as an escape is likely to be speech devoid of serious content and full of ego.

Saint Benedict forbids laughter. This is startling, because among the most valuable members of any community are the cheerful people who can get others to laugh or to smile. Even practical jokers have a contribution to make. Perhaps Benedict was thinking of raucous laughter, or laughter at the expense of others, or laughter at off-color jokes, all of which may be implied by the Latin words he uses for "laughter." Certainly laughter, like silence and speech, can be used for purposes of ridicule and unhealthy social control. However, a genuine smile is almost always a grace, and an occasional all-out laugh can be very therapeutic.

Benedict was insistent that monks listen to each other. The abbot should not make decisions without consulting his advisers or even the whole community. Monks were to listen to the abbot, since he held the place of the Lord Christ among them. Elders were to lend understanding ears to the troubles of the neophytes and other members of the community. All were to listen respectfully to the ideas of the young, because God often reveals the best course of action to them. The applications of these admonitions beyond the monastery are obvious enough. The way to find out if we are really listening is to ask those who speak to us.

Listening requires selectivity. We should avoid gossip and chatter, flattery and deception, detraction and slander. Putting down others so that one might rise is a much-used strategy, and one that leaves speaker, listener, and victim violated. Syncletica was eloquent on the need to avoid malicious and quarrelsome talk.

Speech should arise from humility. It should be at the service of truth. From a truthful heart should come truthful words. Each of us should have someone with whom we can be completely honest about ourselves. The truths about ourselves that we conceal from everyone destroy our inner peace.

Complaining corrodes community life. Humility is one hedge against complaining: few of us deserve what we have, much less have a right to more. Some complaining is objectively justified and would not occur if there were legitimate avenues of communication through which people could make problems and difficulties known and find solutions to them. In fact, there are times when silence is sinful. One must speak up to protect the innocent or abused, to try to correct those who are wrecking their lives, to defend the truth from falsehood, to report that the king is wearing no clothes. An honest argument is better than passive-aggressive silence.

If the highest use of speech is the praise of God, teaching others cannot rank far behind. The monastic tradition emphasizes the superior's duty to teach by both word and example. Surely the same duty applies to every teacher, every parent, every mentor. Louis de Blois warns us: before giving an answer or advice, pray to God for guidance, then speak humbly, prudently, and wisely. Never answer harshly.

Some brothers were coming from Scetis to see Abba Antony. As they were boarding a boat to go there, they found an old man who also wanted to go there. The brothers did not know him. They sat in the boat, occupied by turns with the words of the Fathers, Scripture and their manual work. The old man remained silent. When they arrived at the place to disembark, they found that the old man was going to the cell of Abba Antony too. When they reached the place, Antony said to them, "You found this old man a good companion for the journey?" Then he said to the old man, "You have brought many good brethren with you, father." The old man said, "Certainly they are good, but there is no door on their house, and anyone can enter the stable and untie the ass." He meant that the brethren said whatever came into their mouths.

ANTONY, *SAYINGS*

Again the Spirit teaches the tongue its own purity, since the tongue is very sick. . . . But the mind is strengthened by the Spirit; first it is purified, then it learns discretion in the words it delivers to the tongue so that they are free of hypocrisy and self-will.

ANTONY, *LETTERS*

[Pachomius] called Theodore and said to him, "When the brothers come out from table in the evening, give your ministry to someone else and come to where we gather for the instruction on Sunday." And when Theodore came to the instruction, he told him, "Stand here in the midst of the brothers and speak the word of God to us"—as he used to do himself. He obeyed and stood up, though unwillingly, and he began to speak what the Lord gave him. All stood, including Abba Pachomius who listened as one of them. But some, out of pride, were vexed and they returned to their tents so as not to listen to him. The one who stood [to speak] was younger in human age.

After the instruction and prayer Pachomius sat down as was his custom and he began saying, "You have heard what was said. Whose was it? The speaker's or the Lord's? And those who were vexed, for what reason were they vexed? Because he is younger? But we find that the Lord said about a child, 'Anyone who receives a child like this in my name receives me.' Was I not standing and listening as one of you? And I tell you that I did not only pretend but I was listening with all my heart, as one thirsty for water. For worthy indeed of all acceptance is the word of the Lord, as it is written. Wretched are those who went away; they have estranged themselves from God's mercies."

LIFE OF PACHOMIUS

In the monastery of Phbow there were ten ancient brothers who, although they were chaste in body, often used to murmur and would not listen to the Man of God [Pachomius] with faith. Since he was patient and loved their souls, especially the ones for whom he had been toiling for a long time, admonishing and exhorting them, he did not want to neglect them. He mourned for them before the Lord, humbling his soul with fasting, spending six days without food and up to forty nights without sleep. And his body became extremely lean and feeble. Then the Lord heard him and each one of them received the understanding to be healed from his error as much as possible.

LIFE OF PACHOMIUS

Moreover, by closing her senses as if they were windows, Syncletica continued to converse in solitude with her bridegroom, referring to the following passage: "I belong to my beloved and my beloved belongs to me." If conversations of a questionable and unedifying nature were taking place, she avoided them, retreating to the inner treasure chambers of her soul; but where enlightened and helpful counsels were being offered, she concentrated her whole mind on receiving what was being said.

LIFE OF SYNCLETICA

Malicious talk, therefore, is a serious and troublesome matter, for it is the sustenance and recreation of some people. You should not, however, accept empty hearsay, lest you become a receptacle for other peoples' evils. Keep your own soul unlittered. For, by accepting the foul-smelling garbage of words, you will introduce stains to your prayer through your thoughts, and without cause you will hate your associates. For when your hearing has been drenched with the misanthropy of malicious talkers, you will look on all people without generosity, just as the eye has a blurred image of objects when it is inordinately obsessed with color.

LIFE OF SYNCLETICA

There is no need, then, to be quarrelsome. Do not spend long periods of time in extended conversations, for the Devil can actually do harm through inopportune chitchat.

LIFE OF SYNCLETICA

Listen, O child, to the commands of your master, and bend
the ear of your heart.

RULE OF BENEDICT

With our eyes open to the deifying light and our ears at-
tuned, let us hear the divine voice that calls to us each day
and admonishes us: "If today you hear his voice, do not
harden your hearts."

RULE OF BENEDICT

Offer advice with all the deference of humility, and do not
presume to defend your point of view obstinately.

RULE OF BENEDICT

Utter truth from the heart and from the mouth.

RULE OF BENEDICT

Be neither a complainer nor a detractor.

RULE OF BENEDICT

Reveal to a spiritual elder evil thoughts that come to
your heart.

RULE OF BENEDICT

Keep your mouth from evil or depraved talk, do not love
much talking, do not talk mindlessly or in a way that
prompts laughter, do not love much or violent laughter.

RULE OF BENEDICT

Confess to God daily with tears and sighs your past sins,
and correct them for the future.

RULE OF BENEDICT

Do not wish to be called holy before you are.

RULE OF BENEDICT

To be silent and to listen befits the disciple.

RULE OF BENEDICT

The ninth step of humility is that the monk forbid his tongue to speak, and keeping quiet, not speak unless he is asked a question. . . . The tenth step of humility is that one not be quick and ready to laugh, because it is written: "The fool raises his voice in laughter." The eleventh step of humility is that when a monk speaks, he does so gently and without laughter, and that he speaks few and reasonable words humbly, with restraint.

RULE OF BENEDICT

If any brother is found to be defiant or disobedient or proud or murmuring or in some other way contravening the holy rule and the commands of his seniors, then, in accord with our Lord's command, he should be admonished a first and second time secretly by his seniors. If he will not amend, let him be corrected publicly.

RULE OF BENEDICT

Monks should strive for silence at all times, but especially during the night. . . . Exceptions to this may arise from the needs of guests or from a command of the abbot, but these should be taken care of with the utmost seriousness and gentle restraint.

RULE OF BENEDICT

If a visiting monk . . . reasonably and with loving humility singles out something in the community for criticism, the abbot should prudently consider the matter, because the Lord may have sent the visitor for this very purpose.

RULE OF BENEDICT

At the gate of the monastery there should be a wise old man who knows how to receive a message and respond, one whose age will keep him from wandering. This porter

should have a room near the gate, so that those who come
to the monastery will always find there someone who can
respond to them. As soon as anyone knocks or a poor man
calls, let him respond: "Thanks be to God," or "Bless you";
and let him answer him promptly with all the kindness of
the fear of God and with the fervor of charity.

RULE OF BENEDICT

If anyone . . . senses that a superior or anyone else is irritated
or angry with him, even slightly, let him immediately lie flat
on the ground before his feet making satisfaction, until the
disturbance is cured by a blessing.

RULE OF BENEDICT

I would like you to take a few moments to consider what
our pride does. When we notice that some of the mysteries
of the Scriptures that . . . we have learned with the Lord's
help and that we are discussing are beyond the grasp of some
of the more simple brethren, we are likely to immediately
extol ourselves and look down on them. We take pride in
our almost unique and wide-ranging learning, as if there
were not many people much more learned than we whom
we do not want to despise us. We enjoy ridiculing those
who are less educated than we and make no effort to remember that entry into the kingdom lies open not for those
who only learn the mysteries of faith and the commands of
the Creator by meditating on them, but for those who put
into practice the things they have learned.

BEDE, *HOMILIES ON THE GOSPELS*

Those who conceive the grace of heavenly inspiration in
their mind, those who have learned words of exhortation
by which they are able to comfort their neighbor, must not
hide in silence the good that they know. They should com-
municate it right away to their brothers by speaking
openly.

BEDE, *HOMILIES ON THE GOSPELS*

[As a boy,] Wulfstan rejected, first of all in himself, then in others, foolish talking, which is a source for temptations. He matured so quickly that he gathered boys of his own age and even older boys to pray that by living well they might provide each other the example of a good life. If he did something wrong, they would reprove him; he gladly accepted correction.

LIFE OF WULFSTAN

When Wulfstan noticed that the moral conduct of the people was declining because of lack of preaching, every Sunday and major feast in church, he poured out on them the counsels of salvation.

LIFE OF WULFSTAN

This is surely wisdom: if you live well, if your deeds precede your words.

LIFE OF WULFSTAN

We must not regard with contempt the rebuke of a just man, for such a rebuke is the destruction of sin and a healing for the heart, as well as a path for God to the soul. We should never neglect to listen to any discourse that supports piety, virtues, and good behavior, for it is a way by which the salvation of God is manifested. . . . If you are not only moved to compunction by the conversation, but even converted totally to the Lord, swearing and promising to keep the judgment of his justice, you will also know that he is already present, especially if you feel yourself burning with his love.

BERNARD OF CLAIRVAUX,
ON THE SONG OF SONGS

If a brother is addicted to some fault, a man of the church who already has received the Spirit will try to instruct him right away in the same spirit of gentleness, keeping an eye on himself lest he fall into the same sin.

BERNARD OF CLAIRVAUX,
ON THE SONG OF SONGS

[In accusing a brother of a fault,] if it is manifest, use the
gentle words of the gentle lamb. . . . If it is hidden, correct
it privately; don't make a public disclosure. If it is a powerful
person or prelate, follow the example of Nathan's correction
of David and Noah's two sons: proceed cautiously and indirectly.

PETER OF CELLE,
THE SCHOOL OF THE CLOISTER

Silence is neither mute nor talkative. . . . In such silence
holy desires, peace and calm of heart, and true purity
grow and multiply, in the absence of windy and vain talka-
tiveness . . . which sows discord.

PETER OF CELLE,
THE SCHOOL OF THE CLOISTER

[There are seven reasons for silence:] tranquillity, profession,
peace, to subdue feelings and inclinations of the heart, to
detach oneself from secular affairs, to study the law of God,
for the sake of contemplation.

PETER OF CELLE,
THE SCHOOL OF THE CLOISTER

True confession omits nothing, for in it one accuses oneself
of all excesses both of the flesh and of higher reason. It is
one thing to sin by the senses, which you have in common
with the animal kingdom; it is another to sin by reason,
which you have as proper to your humanity. . . . Sins of the
senses are those that arise from weakness or surprise, for
which you owe a lesser penalty and penance. Sins of the
reason, which occur from deliberation and ambition, are
subject to the more stringent penalty.

PETER OF CELLE,
THE SCHOOL OF THE CLOISTER

Here the human heart can be in possession of itself, for it
has narrowed all questions to one. Having excluded all that
is alien, your heart must devote its attention to its own

affairs. That one question is great, but not insoluble, if you always zealously seek yourself in God and God in yourself. However, there is a preliminary question: to seek yourself in yourself. . . . Our solitary inquiry goes better in silence and is studied more deeply in solitude.

PETER OF CELLE,
ON AFFLICTION AND READING

Falsehood does not rejoice with the truth, but exaggerates about what is not and cannot be, and it does this with exaltation and unjust happiness. Falsehood tells no one the truth, but tells lies about strange things that no one could see. Falsehood tries to do this against God and his saints, in whom God works many miracles. That a person sins in fleshly desires is human, but when he resorts to lying he is inhuman. For lies entangle themselves with more lies, like a snake hiding itself in its lair.

HILDEGARD OF BINGEN,
BOOK OF LIFE'S MERITS

However, since it is almost inhuman for a person to be silent always and never speak, the same father [Benedict] left this matter, as he did many other things, in the power of the judgment of the abbot. He may provide a suitable time for the disciples to speak together about matters that are good and necessary, so that they will not be burdened with weariness because of excessive silence.

HILDEGARD OF BINGEN,
EXPLANATION OF THE RULE OF BENEDICT

If Gertrude had an opportunity to give some advice or suggestion to someone, she put aside all her usual modesty (a virtue that shone brilliantly among all her other virtues) and ignored all inordinate human respect. Confident in him who had armed her with the faith and to whom she wanted to subject the universe, she dipped the pen of her tongue in the blood of her heart, and fashioned words filled with such great love and profound wisdom that the most hardened and contrary people, if there was a spark of piety in them, felt themselves touched by what they heard, at least to the extent that they conceived the will or desire to amend.

GERTRUDE THE GREAT,
THE HERALD OF DIVINE LOVE

We are going to render an account to God, not only for our idle words, but also for our ill-considered silence.

JOHN TRITHEMIUS, *RULE*

For the devout mind, the first cause of ruin is lack of attention. . . . The cause of all evil is a negligent heart.

JOHN TRITHEMIUS, *RULE*

If anyone seeks advice from you, recognize in your heart that you cannot give a suitable answer on your own. Turn to God and pray silently: "O Lord God, who are in me, deign to speak through me whatever pleases you and is most suited to your honor and the salvation of souls." Then say humbly, prudently, and wisely whatever should be said. If you have spoken well, attribute that to God; if badly, ascribe that to yourself. At all times avoid unseasonable harshness in your speech. Be truthful in speech, and avoid both false show and flattery. Do not be eager to say anything that blames others.

LOUIS DE BLOIS, *SPIRITUAL DOCTRINE*

In speaking, be circumspect, polite, restrained, and without fault. Love reasonable silence. Do not say things that are utterly vain or useless, and that arouse unbridled laughter. . . . Avoid excessively sharp and biting words, and abominate the vice of detraction and slander. . . . Also, do not affirm as certain anything that you do not know for sure. . . . If it should happen that you hear someone saying mocking or wicked or unkind words, end the conversation politely, or even modestly and discretely correct the one who was speaking.

LOUIS DE BLOIS, *SPIRITUAL MIRROR*

Have a special love for solitude, silence, and restraint in speech. Always be more ready to listen to talking than to utter it. Don't be impatient, unruly, loud, or contentious in your words, but say true and proper things without any deception and modestly, humbly, and with goodwill.

LOUIS DE BLOIS, *SPIRITUAL MIRROR*

Conferences about spiritual matters are very useful; they have been held in religious communities from the beginning. There are two kinds. One sort consists in talks given by superiors to their subjects; the other consists in conversations among religious regarding matters of piety. . . . This sort of conference is no longer held in communities, but one could usefully reestablish it. Such conferences might be no less advantageous than the conferences given by superiors. . . . Let me indicate my thoughts about reestablishing this holy practice and propose two or three ways of conducting such conferences. . . . The first would be to undertake in common the reading of some important material . . . and to let each have the freedom to indicate what difficulties he found in the reading. . . . The second method would be to propose subjects or materials for conferences for the entire year or one by one. . . . A third method, no less useful, is that a qualified religious give a lecture on some determined subject, and that he respond to questions proposed to him.

JEAN MABILLON,
TREATISE ON THE STUDIES OF MONKS

To live in communion, in genuine dialogue with others is absolutely necessary if man is to remain human. But to live in the midst of others, sharing nothing with them but the common noise and the general distraction, isolates a man in the worst way, separates him from reality in a way that is almost painless.

THOMAS MERTON,
NEW SEEDS OF CONTEMPLATION

"Listen!" I could take that as a summary of the whole of
Benedict's teaching. I could spend the rest of my life pondering on the implications of that one word. It plunges
me at once into a personal relationship. It takes me away
from the danger of talking about God and not communing
with him.

ESTHER DE WAAL, *A LIFE-GIVING WAY*

[The three moments of the Prodigal's way back to his Father
are] first the listening and responding, obedience (for that
is what the word means, *obaudiens,* to listen intently), then
the *metanoia,* or turning (which is what *conversatio morum*
involves, continual conversion, journeying on), and then
the stability (from the Latin *stare,* to stand), being in the
place of firm ground.

ESTHER DE WAAL, *A LIFE-GIVING WAY*

Anyone who loves words will tend to let themselves be
satisfied by them, and as a result stop short of true satisfaction. For true satisfaction . . . comes when I am silent and
listen. . . . When God's voice is drowned out by incessant
clamor, whether inner or outer, in whatever shape or form,
then continuous dialogue with God becomes impossible.
An inner monologue with myself, constant chatter with
others, the invasion of the spoken word through the press
and television are all the ever-present realities in my daily
life over which I need to exercise some sort of discipline if
I am to keep any quiet inner space in which to listen to the
Word.

ESTHER DE WAAL, *A LIFE-GIVING WAY*

Speaking is something that must be undertaken reverently
and responsibly. If I reflect on what Benedict is saying, I
find guidelines for my own situation. This is not a call for
absolute silence (silence can after all become an instrument
of the passive aggressive, and it can be isolating, hurtful), but

for a restrained, disciplined, and thoughtful approach to
speech.

ESTHER DE WAAL, *A LIFE-GIVING WAY*

Clearly, for Benedict, God is not something to be achieved;
God is a presence to be responded to but to whom, without
that presence, we cannot respond.

ESTHER DE WAAL, *A LIFE-GIVING WAY*

The end of Benedictine spirituality is to develop a transpar-
ent personality. Dissimulation, half answers, vindictive atti-
tudes, a false presentation of self are all barbs in the soul of
the monastic. Holiness, this ancient rule says to a culture
that has made crafty packaging high art, has something to do
with being who we say we are, claiming our truths, opening
our hearts, giving ourselves to the other pure and unglossed.

SR. JOAN CHITTISTER,
THE RULE OF BENEDICT

Silence is a cornerstone of Benedictine life and spiritual
development, but the goal of monastic silence is not non-
talking. The goal of monastic silence and monastic speech
is respect for others, a sense of place, a spirit of peace. . . .
Silence for its own selfish, insulating sake, silence that is
passive-aggressive, silence that is insensitive to the present
needs of the other is not Benedictine silence.

SR. JOAN CHITTISTER,
THE RULE OF BENEDICT

Humor and laughter are not necessarily the same thing.
Humor permits us to see into life from a fresh and gracious
perspective. We learn to take ourselves more lightly in the
presence of good humor. Humor gives us the strength
to bear what cannot be changed, and the sight to see the
human under the pompous.

SR. JOAN CHITTISTER,
THE RULE OF BENEDICT

CHAPTER 7

Reverence

"Fear of the Lord is the beginning of wisdom" (Prv 1.7) is an often repeated assertion of the sages of the Old Testament. The *Rule of Benedict,* which borrows much from the sages' writings, reiterates the same truth. On the one hand, Benedict urges the monk to find Christ in the needy guest and neighbor, but at the same time Benedict warns that God and Christ know our every thought and action and will judge us from them. It is difficult to know which aspect of Benedict's Christology is more demanding and more frightful.

Fear of the Lord is not a sentiment widely acknowledged in our society. For us, God is a merciful God, and nothing more need be said. Hell has become an abstract possibility, not a threatening reality. Our convictions about divine mercy are surely justified by the New Testament. However, a God who is completely and merely merciful is neither just nor justifying. Before such a God, human responsibility does not seem to count for much. Benedict takes God and the possibility of hell very seriously.

A useful first step in dealing with this wide difference between Benedict's *Rule* and modern religious sentiment is to note that the fear Benedict has in mind seems to be closely connected with reverence. Benedict wants his monks to be reverent toward God, reverent toward the community and its possessions, reverent toward visitors. In a passage quoted in conjunction with Benedict's teaching on prayer, Gregory the Great reports that Benedict once saw a vision of the whole world in a single sunbeam. Gregory draws the conclusion that to one who has seen God, the world appears to be very small. Perhaps. However, Benedict seems to have found the world and all that it is in it sacred, worthy of care and cultivation, too precious to claim as one's own property. Benedict does not contrast the sacredness of church space and church time to the insignificance of secular places and secular activities. His inclination is to extend the reverence one should feel in liturgical settings to the whole of reality. Hence Hildegard's declaration that all of God's creatures are pleasing and none should be injured.

After God, it is human beings who deserve our honor. All human beings—elderly, young, strangers or neighbors, the productive and the seemingly unproductive.

Had I chosen to discuss chastity, this would probably be the place to do it. For chastity, whether celibate or married, is very much a matter of reverence for ourselves and for other persons embodied and alluring, whom we are tempted to possess or control and so to violate. For the monk or nun, sexual relations are one path to God not taken because they have chosen other paths instead. That said, the thesis of this book is that the paths to God of monk and non-monk are very much alike. As one friend of mine said: husband and wife become each other's monastery. Their life together is a sacrament, holy to the church because of what it teaches about faithfulness and steadfastness and compassion and holy hilarity and tenderness and hospitality and the sanctity of everyday things. Their marriage is a continual conversion to their life together, to listening to one another, to care of one another and others.

Honor all people, and do not do to another what you do not want to happen to yourself.

RULE OF BENEDICT

Venerate the elders; love the younger people.

RULE OF BENEDICT

The first degree of humility is "to keep the fear of God always before one's eyes" [Ps 36.2], and to avoid all forgetfulness, always mindful of all that God commands. One should

always be pondering in one's mind how hell burns for their
sins those who hold God in contempt, while eternal life has
been prepared for those who fear God.

RULE OF BENEDICT

When the cantor begins to say, "Glory be . . . ," all should
immediately rise from their seats out of respect and reverence for the Holy Trinity.

RULE OF BENEDICT

We believe that God is present everywhere, and that the eyes
of the Lord behold good and evil people everywhere; we
believe this especially without any hesitation when we assist
at the work of God.

RULE OF BENEDICT

When the work of God is finished, all should leave [the
chapel] in deep silence and show reverence for God.

RULE OF BENEDICT

Juniors [in the time of entry into the monastery] should
honor their seniors, and seniors should love their juniors. . . .
Whenever they meet one another, the junior should ask a
blessing from the senior. When a senior walks by, the junior
should rise and give him his seat. The junior should not presume to sit down again unless the senior bids him. Thus,
they may fulfill what is written: "They should strive to
honor one another" [Rom 12.10].

RULE OF BENEDICT

The prior [second-in-command] must perform with reverence whatever is enjoined on him by the abbot and do
nothing against the will or arrangements of the abbot. Just as
he has been placed before others, so it is required of him
that he observe the precepts of the rule more carefully.

RULE OF BENEDICT

The first glimpse of wisdom is fear of the Lord, just as the dawn precedes the sun. For when a person understands that she has been created by God, she begins to fear God. What is feared is honored, and what is honored is loved; if it is loved rightly, it is also honored rightly.

HILDEGARD OF BINGEN,
BOOK OF LIFE'S MERITS

Reverence declares: "All the things God established please me. I do not hurt any of them."

HILDEGARD OF BINGEN,
BOOK OF LIFE'S MERITS

As [Benedict's *Rule*] says: "When the work of God is finished, let all go out with the greatest silence; and let a reverence be made to God" [*Rule of Benedict* 55.2]. Let them bow reverently as they go out, and let them have reverence in their other works that are done in the service of God, and not rush into anything wanton or excessive.

HILDEGARD OF BINGEN,
EXPLANATION OF THE RULE OF BENEDICT

[Gertrude's] tender compassion extended not only to human beings, but reached out to every creature. When she saw little birds or other animals suffering from hunger, thirst, or cold, she was moved with intense pity for the work of her Lord. Then, desiring that God have mercy on his creature and deign to relieve its misery, she strove to offer devoutly to the Lord's eternal praise this suffering of irrational creation, in union with the dignity by which every creature is supremely perfected and ennobled in God.

GERTRUDE THE GREAT,
THE HERALD OF DIVINE LOVE

There is this difference between filial and servile fear: the child fears to offend; the servant shudders at the thought of being whipped. Filial fear is virtuous because it shows reverence for one's parent; servile fear is good, because it shows forth the power of the Lord. However, it is better to have filial fear and love than to fear and fail to love.

JOHN TRITHEMIUS, *RULE*

In the midst of the multiple activities of the day, you should stay free of multiplicity and preserve oneness of spirit within yourself. Let your mind form an idea of God and of his supreme majesty and goodness. Keep his lovable presence before your mind's eye.

LOUIS DE BLOIS, *SPIRITUAL DOCTRINE*

It was because the saints were absorbed in God that they were truly capable of seeing and appreciating created things and it was because they loved Him alone that they alone loved everybody.

THOMAS MERTON,
NEW SEEDS OF CONTEMPLATION

[Benedict] writes about the elderly and children and about their need for special understanding. . . . When society seems increasingly to say that productivity and usefulness are the qualities by which we judge the worth of the individual, here Benedict is telling us that respect should be shown to those who apparently contribute little or nothing to the community in these terms.

ESTHER DE WAAL, *A LIFE-GIVING WAY*

Benedict has a deep belief and respect for each one of us as sons and daughters made in the image of God. It is up to each of us to take due and proper responsibility for the handling of this amazing gift of our sonship or daughterhood.

ESTHER DE WAAL, *A LIFE-GIVING WAY*

[Benedict] knew that the secret of the holy life was not so much a holy reputation as it was a holy attitude toward all of creation: reverence for God, reverence for the body,

reverence for the other who is younger and unimportant,
or older and useless now, or in opposition to us and an irri-
tant now.

SR. JOAN CHITTISTER,
THE RULE OF BENEDICT

In a society that depends on reputation to such a degree that
people build themselves up by tearing other people down,
the chapter on mutual obedience turns the world awry.
Monastic spirituality says that we are to honor one another.
We are to listen to one another. We are to reach across
boundaries and differences in this fragmented world and see
in our differences distinctions of great merit that can mend a
competitive, uncaring, and foolish world.

SR. JOAN CHITTISTER,
THE RULE OF BENEDICT

CHAPTER 8

Humility

Saint Antony saw the world as something like a minefield that only humility can safely traverse. Benedict's teaching on humility is also a difficult minefield for interpreters. I do not know that a person can or should think he is lower and baser than all others (Benedict's seventh degree of humility). Humility is truth. In truth, it is statistically very unlikely that anyone is the lowest of all. Nor do I think we should work at looking humble (twelfth degree of humility). Humility is truth. One should not try to appear as anything, least of all as a foot-shuffling nobody.

Antony and Benedict knew that a true monk could accept insults and humiliations, in part because he deserved them, but, I suspect, also because they knew that a truly humble person cannot be humiliated. Someone who knows her own weaknesses and accepts them will not be terrified by the prospect of humiliations. Someone who does not pretend to be anything other than what she is will not be afraid of what people say about her.

Merton saw clearly that the ultimate basis of humility is grace: whatever one is or has or accomplishes is a gift from God and others. As the Eucharist is the offering of God's gifts back to God, so monastic life and any Christian life is an offering of God's gift of oneself to God.

Bede's homilies are thoroughly Christological. He is particularly given to citing the incarnation of the Son of God in the humanity of Christ as a supreme example of humility. For Christ, humbling himself was a way to share the lives of his human brothers and sisters. For us, humility is an acknowledgment that we share the weaknesses and the sins of our human brothers and sisters. Humility is also a recognition that we form one living system with the plants and animals, for all physical things, living and dead, arise ultimately from the *humus,* the moist ground of virgin earth. Try as we may to forget it, we will always need to share water and air and sunlight with the plants and the animals.

Humility is an essential part of listening. Only someone who believes he has something to learn is an attentive listener. The *Life of Pachomius* tells about Silvanos, who learned humility by imitating and obeying a humble man, and in that way Silvanos became "a living man." The beast of pride, which wars against each of us, Silvanos slew.

Humility is not about comparisons with other people, but if we are inclined to make too much of our virtues or achievements, we should remind ourselves of how many people have been able to exceed any accomplishment of ours. The more we know ourselves, the more we discover we are lower than our image of ourselves. In knowing ourselves and avoiding making comparisons between ourselves and those we know less well, we should be ready to do them any service or accept any assignment. Christ did the same.

Because humility avoids comparison, envy is a sure sign of its absence. Humility can rejoice in the gifts of all, because it recognizes the fundamental oneness of all people in their humanity and in Christ. Envy thinks of gifts as private property. Not only did Gertrude not think of her gifts as private property; she thought they were given her only so she might pass them on to others.

When a person has walked consciously in the presence of God and with God's help discovered how merciful God has been to him even in his sin, that person loves God more and more until this love casts out fear. For Benedict, love overcame and cast out fear not because he came to believe there was no hell, but because he discovered how good God had been to him and he had no reason to think God would ever act differently toward him. Fear helps keep us on the straight and narrow during the early and laborious days of our seeking to become what God wills for us. As we acquire virtue, we come more and more to do the good spontaneously out of good habit, delight in virtue, and love of Christ.

Humility is the truth about ourselves, the whole truth—about our weaknesses, our failures, our history, our virtues, our gifts. Once we are truthful about ourselves before God and others, we can deal gently with others who are afraid to face the truth about themselves or who fancy themselves our competitors. Christ humbled himself out of compassion; out of humility grows our compassion for one another.

[Abba Antony said:] I have seen all the snares of the enemy spread out over the world, and I said with a groan, "Who can get through such snares?" Then I heard a voice say to me, "Humility."

ANTONY, *SAYINGS*

The brothers praised a monk before Abba Antony. When he had received the monk, Antony wanted to learn how he would bear insults. When he saw that he could not bear them at all, he said to him, "You are like a building magnificently decorated on the outside, but pillaged within by robbers."

ANTONY, *SAYINGS*

Therefore, let this word be clear to you: you are not to think that your progress and entry into God's service has been your own work, but rather understand that you have always been helped by a divine power. Strive to offer yourself as a sacrifice to God always.

ANTONY, *LETTERS*

Except through humility in your whole heart and mind and spirit and soul and body, you will not be able to inherit the Kingdom of God.

ANTONY, *LETTERS*

Therefore, Jesus emptied himself of his glory, and took upon himself the form of a slave [Phil 2.7–8], that his bondage might make us free. And we became foolish, and in our foolishness committed every kind of evil. Again, He took the form of foolishness, that by his foolishness we might be made wise.

ANTONY, *LETTERS*

And so I also, the poor wretch who writes this letter, having been awakened from the sleep of death, have spent most of the time I have been upon earth mourning and weeping, saying "What can I render to the Lord for all the benefits he has done for me?" For nothing is lacking to us which he has not done for us in our humiliation.

ANTONY, *LETTERS*

One of the brothers asked me, "Tell us about one of your visions," and I said to him, "A sinner like me does not ask God to see visions." It is against God's will and a mistake. But in everything he does by God's will, even if he should raise a dead man, the servant of God remains unhurt by pride or boasting. For without God's permission, he would not even see that Providence governs all things.

LIFE OF PACHOMIUS

One day [Pachomius] was weaving a mat in Tabennesi. A boy who was doing the weekly service in the monastery came by, and seeing him weaving said, "Not so, father. Do not turn the thread this way, for Abba Theodore has taught us another way of weaving." He got up at once and said, "Yes, teach me the way." After the boy had taught him, he sat down to work with joy, having forestalled the spirit of pride in this, too.

LIFE OF PACHOMIUS

There was a boy called Silvanos. Our father Pachomius had given him instructions before receiving him into the monastery, but afterwards Silvanos became negligent. . . . Pachomius was patient with him; he called a great monk named Psenamon and told him in the boy's absence, "We know that you have labored in ascesis for a long time. Now, for God's sake, take this boy and suffer with him in all things until he is saved.". . . And so they worked together making mats, and they fulfilled the fast and the prayers properly. The boy obeyed Psenamon in everything as he had been commanded. He would not eat even a vegetable leaf without asking. And so he was humble, great [in virtue] and meek, keeping his mouth closed. . . . And to say it in short, he became a living man.

One day when the brothers were seated, Abba Pachomius began to tell them, "There is a man among us as I have not seen ever since I became a monk. . . . By his deep humility and the purity of his conscience he is great. The beast that wars against you, you have bound and put under your feet; and if you are negligent it will be set loose again and rise up against you. But Silvanos has slain it."

LIFE OF PACHOMIUS

Even if you were . . . successfully practicing the most extreme asceticism, do not make too much of it! For demons have in fact done and are doing more ascetic acts than yours. They do not eat, nor drink, nor sleep. They also spend their lives in a desert—in case you think that you are doing something great by living in a cave.

LIFE OF SYNCLETICA

So great a virtue is humility that, although the Devil seems to mimic all virtues, he does not begin to understand the nature of this one. . . . Just as it is impossible for a ship to be built without nails, so it is impossible to be saved without humility.

LIFE OF SYNCLETICA

Because humility is good and salutary, the Lord clothed himself in it while fulfilling the work of salvation [economy] for humanity. For he says: "Learn from me, for I am gentle and humble of heart" [Mt 11.29]. Notice who it is who is speaking. Learn his lesson perfectly. Let humility become for you

the beginning and end of virtues. He means a humble heart.
He refers not to appearance alone, but to the inner person,
for the outer person will also follow after the inner.

LIFE OF SYNCLETICA

Humility, then, is formed through rebukes, through insults,
through blows; you hear yourself called mindless and stupid,
poor and a beggar, weak and worthless, ineffectual in what
you do and irrational in what you say, contemptible in appearance, weak in power. These insults are the sinews of humility. These our Lord heard and experienced, for they said
he was a Samaritan and was possessed. He took on the form
of a slave, he was beaten, he was humiliated with blows.

LIFE OF SYNCLETICA

They know that what is good in themselves could not have
come about except for the Lord. They heap praise on the
Lord working in them, saying with the prophet: "Not to us,
Lord, not to us, but to your name give the glory" [Ps 115.1].

RULE OF BENEDICT

The sixth step of humility is that a monk is content with
every sort of mean and extreme condition, and judges himself a bad and unworthy worker in all the things that are enjoined upon him.

RULE OF BENEDICT

The seventh degree of humility is that one not only says
with his tongue but believes with the deepest feeling of his
heart that he is lower and baser than all others.

RULE OF BENEDICT

The twelfth degree of humility is that a monk always shows
himself to be humble not only in his heart but also to those
who see the way he carries himself at the work of God, in
the chapel, in the monastery, in the garden, on the road, in
the field, wherever he sits, walks, or stands. With his head always down, his eyes on the ground, at every moment think-

ing himself guilty of his sins, let him consider himself to be
already presented before the fearful judgment, always saying
to himself in his heart what the publican in the Gospels said
with his eyes fixed on the ground: "Lord, I, a sinner, am not
worthy to raise my eyes to the heavens."

RULE OF BENEDICT

Having ascended all these steps of humility, the monk will
soon arrive at that perfect love of God that casts out fear,
through which all those things that previously he did not
observe without fear he will begin to keep effortlessly, as
though practice had made them second nature, no longer
out of fear of hell, but out of love for Christ, and good habit
and delight in virtues. These things the Lord will deign to
show by the Holy Spirit in his workman now cleansed of
vices and sins.

RULE OF BENEDICT

Since, when we wish to propose something to powerful persons, we do not presume to do so except with humility and
reverence, how much more ought we petition the Lord God
of all things with all humility and pure devotion.

RULE OF BENEDICT

[Priests in the community] should give a better example of
humility than anyone else.

RULE OF BENEDICT

The physician [Christ] came to visit the sick. In order to
heal the chronic weakness of our pride, he offered us the
fresh example of his humility.

BEDE, HOMILIES ON THE GOSPELS

Although Wulfstan excelled all others in virtues, he
showed humility toward each person. He was constantly
doing menial tasks that another would have found dis-
gusting.

LIFE OF WULFSTAN

Certain ones said that the humility he loved was beneath the dignity of a bishop. Wulfstan answered: "Whoever is the greatest among you will be your servant. I am your bishop and teacher; therefore I must be the servant of you all, according to the Lord's command."

LIFE OF WULFSTAN

See, blessed Benedict, how vigorously this soldier of Christ fights under your leadership! See how effectively this student of yours advances in your school. See the good monk who, having mortified his evil ways and fleshly desires, is so eager and lives solely for virtue. No! Behold a false monk who, having lost the virtues, is ruled by a crowd of vices and smothered under a heap of sins!

ANSELM OF CANTERBURY,
PRAYERS AND MEDITATIONS

Many of those who are humiliated are not humble. Some react to humiliation with anger, others with patience, and others with freedom. The first are culpable, the next harmless, the last just. While innocence is part of justice, its consummation is found in the humble. The humble person who can say "It is good for me that you humbled me" is really humble. Someone who bears humiliation unwillingly cannot say this, much less someone who complains. We promise no grace to either of these because of their humiliation. Nevertheless, the two are quite different: one will possess his soul in patience; the other will perish in his complaining. Although one arouses anger, neither merits grace, for it is not to the humiliated but to the humble that God gives grace.

BERNARD OF CLAIRVAUX,
ON THE SONG OF SONGS

When people are proud, they envy the accomplishments of others and then stir up every kind of evil.

HILDEGARD OF BINGEN,
BOOK OF LIFE'S MERITS

[In her humility, Gertrude] thought herself so unworthy of God's gifts that she could not accept that they might be for her benefit alone. Instead, she saw herself as a channel through whom grace could flow to God's elect by the mysterious ways of Providence.

GERTRUDE THE GREAT,
THE HERALD OF DIVINE LOVE

Since my tongue is incapable of recounting the abundant favors you have given me by the continuous gift of your presence, accept, I beg you, O my God, the sentiment of my heart. From the depths of the abyss of humility where I have been gently drawn by your downward-bending charity, grant me to recognize and render thanks to your infinite goodness.

GERTRUDE THE GREAT,
THE HERALD OF DIVINE LOVE

Vainglory is a love of our own excellence. Vainglory gives birth to self-exaltation, pride, arrogance, contention, affront, contempt, presumption, disobedience, irreverence, and very often to factions, the worst of plagues. To avoid these things, we must glory in the Lord and not in ourselves.

JOHN TRITHEMIUS, *RULE*

Our Teacher . . . appeared with the humble, for he was the most humble of all. Let us remain in his teaching. Whatever he taught by word and example, let us fulfill by deed.

JOHN TRITHEMIUS, *RULE*

Have a humble and submissive heart. Acknowledge your nothingness, your weakness and lack of power. Acknowledge your ingratitude toward God, your wickedness and vileness. . . . Attribute to the mercy and kindness of God whatever good you have and do; in this, seek not your own praise and glory but God's. . . . Forgive from

your heart every offense of those who trouble you or injure
you.

LOUIS DE BLOIS, *SPIRITUAL MIRROR*

The things we really need come to us only as gifts, and in
order to receive them as gifts we have to be open. In order
to be open we have to renounce ourselves, in a sense we
have to die to our image of ourselves, our autonomy, our
fixation upon our self-willed identity.

THOMAS MERTON,
CONJECTURES OF A GUILTY BYSTANDER

A humble man is not disturbed by praise. Since he is no
longer concerned with himself, and since he knows
where the good that is in him comes from, he does not
refuse praise, because it belongs to the God he loves,
and in receiving it he keeps nothing for himself but gives
it all, with great joy, to his God.

THOMAS MERTON,
NEW SEEDS OF CONTEMPLATION

A humble man can do great things with an uncommon perfection because he is no longer concerned about incidentals,
like his own interests and his own reputation, and therefore
he no longer needs to waste his efforts in defending them.

THOMAS MERTON,
NEW SEEDS OF CONTEMPLATION

[Benedict's chapter on humility] is asking of me the honesty
that means that I cease to play games, whether with myself,
with others, with God. Unless I desire this with the whole
of my being, to the extent that I am willing to undergo a
holocaust to achieve it . . . it is hardly worth beginning.

ESTHER DE WAAL, *A LIFE-GIVING WAY*

Lack of contentment lets me become trapped in the coils
of the competitive society, competing for material goods,

social status, the sort of car I drive, the place in which I
live.

ESTHER DE WAAL, *A LIFE-GIVING WAY*

If I accept myself as ordinary, weak, frail, in other words,
totally human and totally dependent upon God, then I am
stripped of any sense of being in some way set apart, different, superior. It is then that the genuine, real self may begin
to emerge.

ESTHER DE WAAL, *A LIFE-GIVING WAY*

The key to my growth in humility is that it brings me closer
to God as it subjects me more and more to the pull of the
gravitational force of God's love.

ESTHER DE WAAL, *A LIFE-GIVING WAY*

[Humility is] a proper sense of self in a universe of wonders.

SR. JOAN CHITTISTER,
THE RULE OF BENEDICT

Benedict wants us to realize that accepting our essential
smallness and embracing it frees us from the need to lie,
even to ourselves, about our frailties. More than that, it lib-
erates us to respect, revere, and deal gently with others who
have been unfortunate enough to have their own smallness
come obscenely to light.

SR. JOAN CHITTISTER,
THE RULE OF BENEDICT

CHAPTER 9

Simplicity

The *Life of Syncletica* presents a paradox. When Syncletica decided to build, she didn't gather materials from outside sources. Instead, she emptied out what she had within, getting rid of possessions and anti-social emotions. Thus she was able to build a solid tower on a rock foundation. Johannes Tauler, a German mystic of the fourteenth century, said simply: God cannot resist a vacuum. God is drawn irresistibly to a soul emptied out of possessions, pride, and hostility. More prosaically, when Syncletica converted to the monastic life, she gave her possessions to the poor and her body to God. In fact, she realized, everything belonged to God anyway.

The primary inspiration for voluntary Christian poverty has been the example and teaching of Christ and the example of the early church as described in the first chapters of Acts.

Syncletica thinks of possessions as tools for a certain kind of life, a life devoted to pleasure or to keeping up with the neighbors. If we renounce that sort of life, we won't need the tools anymore. Once divested of the tools, we don't need to worry about breaking or losing them. We are free. The one who has unlimited needs is never satisfied. Avarice is insatiable. The one who needs only what is sufficient is seldom in need.

While the Benedictine tradition renounces private property, it insists that the goal is for the community to have and distribute to its members what is necessary. What is necessary varies from person to person. So each does not receive exactly the same amount, though no one should receive anything superfluous.

The monastic tradition is convinced of the goodness of creation. We go to God in and through his world. However, the monastic tradition is of several minds about beauty in buildings, liturgy, and artifacts. Generally, the mainstream of Benedictine spirituality has not rejected the enjoyment of beauty, especially when that beauty is associated with the praise of God. Whatever possessions a monastery or an individual happens to have, they are on loan from Christ. They are to be treated with great respect.

Communal superfluity is no more licit than individual luxury. One of the most important lessons of monastic economy is that one can enjoy beauty in many forms without possessing it.

Monastic apparel is a controversial subject, especially because of historical differences in expectations placed on men and women. The best of the tradition was aimed at avoiding ostentation, the ostentation of fine clothes and the ostentation of rags. Benedict says to wear inexpensive clothes found in your area.

The real riches of the voluntary poor are their shared virtue, itself a gift. In the end, all one can give to God is his gift, oneself, a gift endowed with many gifts. Having offered all to God, one is dependent on God, which is to say, one is thoroughly human.

Upon his parents' death, Antony was left alone with an only sister, who was very young. He was about eighteen or twenty years old at the time and took care of the house and his sister. Less than six months had passed since his parents' death when, as usual, he chanced to be on his way to church. As he was walking along, he collected his thoughts and reflected how the Apostles left everything and followed the Savior [Mt 4.20], also how the people in Acts sold what they had and laid it at the feet of the Apostles for distribution among the needy [Acts 4.35], and what great hope is laid up in heaven for such as these [Eph 1.18]. With these thoughts in his mind, he entered the church. And it so happened that the Gospel was being read . . . in which

the Lord says to the rich man: "If you wish to be perfect,
go sell all that you have and give it to the poor; and come,
follow me and you shall have treasure in heaven" [Mt
19.21]. . . . Antony immediately left the church and
gave to the townspeople the property he had from his fore-
bears. . . . He did not want it to encumber himself or his
sister in any way whatever. He sold all the rest . . . keeping
back only a little for his sister. But once again as he entered
the church, he heard the Lord saying in the Gospel: "Be
not solicitous for the morrow" [Mt 6.34]. He could not
bear to wait longer, but went out and distributed those
things also to the poor. His sister he placed with known
and trusted virgins, giving her to the nuns to be brought
up. Then he himself devoted all his time to ascetic living,
intent on himself and living a life of self-denial near his
own home.

LIFE OF ANTONY

Unless each of you hates earthly possession and renounces it
and all its workings with all his heart, and stretches the hands
of his heart to heaven to the Father of all, he cannot be
saved.

ANTONY, *LETTERS*

[Pachomius] used to teach the brothers not to give heed to
the splendor and the beauty of this world in things like good
food, clothing, a cell, or a book outwardly pleasing to the
eye. "For the beauty of the faithful," he said, "lies in the
commandments of God"; as the psalmist says, "Lord, in
your will grant strength to my beauty" [Ps 30.7]. Although
Joseph was extremely handsome and came to rule over
Egypt, he paid no attention to these perishable things, having chastity for splendor and prudence for power. But others
who took their delight in these things perished by an evil
death, like Ammon and Absalom.

LIFE OF PACHOMIUS

[After distributing all her possessions to the poor, Syncletica said:] I have been judged worthy of a great title. What worthy return shall I make to the giver? I do not have anything. If in the outside world, for the sake of a transitory distinction, people throw away their whole substance, how much more necessary is it for me who have been granted so great a grace to offer my body along with what are regarded as possessions? But why do I talk about giving possessions or body when all that belongs to him? "For the Lord's is the earth and its fullness" [Ps 24.1]. Once she had clothed herself with humility [cf. Col 3.12] by means of these words, she entered upon a solitary life.

LIFE OF SYNCLETICA

Now the construction of buildings is traditionally carried out with materials from without, but Syncletica went about it in the opposite way. She did not gather all her building materials from without, but rather she emptied herself of what was within. For by giving her possessions to the poor, by relinquishing anger and vindictiveness, and by driving away envy and ambition, she built her house on rock, its tower visible from afar and its structure storm proof.

LIFE OF SYNCLETICA

[Voluntary poverty] is good for those women who are able to endure it. For the women who persevere in this condition have suffering in the flesh, but peace in the soul. For just as heavy clothing is washed and bleached by treading and vigorous wringing, so also the strong soul is strengthened to a greater degree through voluntary poverty.

LIFE OF SYNCLETICA

For possessions are the "tools" of a life devoted to pleasure. Take away first the "trade" (i.e., gluttony and soft living), and you will also be able easily to dispense with its material aspect represented by your possessions. For it is difficult, in my opinion, if the "trade" is going on, for the "tools" to be absent. For if a woman has not given up the first, how will she be able to reject the second?

LIFE OF SYNCLETICA

The Enemy, moreover, is more soundly vanquished in the case of those who live without possessions. For he lacks the means to do harm, since the majority of our griefs and trials originate in the removal of possessions. What course of action does he have against those without possessions? None! Can he burn their estates? Impossible! Destroy their livestock? They do not even have any! Lay hands on their dear ones? To these too they long ago said good-bye. And so voluntary poverty is a powerful retribution against the Enemy as well as a precious treasure for the soul.

LIFE OF SYNCLETICA

Let the cellarer regard all the utensils of the monastery and everything that belongs to it as if they were vessels consecrated for the altar. Let him not consider anything as having no importance. He should not burn with avarice, nor be wasteful and squander the goods of the monastery, but let him do all things with moderation and as the abbot bids.

RULE OF BENEDICT

Let all things be common to all, as Scripture [Acts 4.32] says, so that no one should say or presume that anything is his own.

RULE OF BENEDICT

In particular this vice is to be rooted out of the monastery: that anyone . . . have anything at all as his own.

RULE OF BENEDICT

As it is written: distribution was made to each as each had need [Acts 4.35]. We certainly do not mean there should be favoritism, but there should be a consideration for weaknesses. Thus, those who need less should thank God and not be upset, whereas those who need more should be humbled because of their weakness and not exalted by the mercy shown them.

RULE OF BENEDICT

Clothing should be given them suitable to the circumstances and the climate of the place where they live.

RULE OF BENEDICT

They should not worry about the color or quality of their clothes, but be satisfied with what can be found in the area where they live and can be purchased inexpensively.

RULE OF BENEDICT

To completely root out the vice of private ownership, the abbot will need to provide all the things that are necessary: cowl, tunic, sandals, shoes, belt, knife, stylus, needle, hand-kerchief, and writing tablets. In that way, all pretext of want will be eliminated.

RULE OF BENEDICT

[Wulfstan] always avoided every sort of ostentation; even when he was wealthy, he wore only lambskins. So, one day, Geoffrey, bishop of Coutances, good-naturedly criticized him. He showered him with friendly jibes. He asked Wulfstan why he wore lambskins when he could and should have had sable or beaver or fox. Wulfstan answered with good grace that Geoffrey and men schooled in worldly wisdom should use the skins of clever animals; he himself, unaware of trickery, would be content with lambskins. Geoffrey came back at him by saying he should at least wear catskins. Wulfstan answered: "Believe me, we sing 'Lamb of God' more often than we sing 'Cat of God.'" Geoffrey heard this and started laughing, delighted that he had the worst of the jest and that Wulfstan could not be budged.

LIFE OF WULFSTAN

Oh how spacious is that soul, and how privileged in her merits, that she is found both worthy to receive the divine presence into herself and sufficient to contain that presence. She provides spacious walkways for the use of the divine majesty. She is certainly not involved in lawsuits and worldly cares, not a devotee of the stomach or of sensual pleasures, nor is she curious to look around, nor avid to command, nor proud in the power she has. It is necessary that the soul first be empty of all these things, so that it can become the heaven and dwelling place of God. Otherwise, how could she be quiet enough to see that it is God himself? She certainly cannot give herself to envy or rancor, because wisdom will not enter the wicked soul. Hence, it is necessary that she grow and expand so that she is able to receive God. Her expanse is her love, as the Apostle indicates: expand in love [2 Cor 6.13].

BERNARD OF CLAIRVAUX,
ON THE SONG OF SONGS

In affliction, two things should be checked regularly, the manner and the fruit: the manner, so that nothing is in excess; the fruit, so that the effort is not in vain. To afflict oneself without measure is tyranny; to do so without fruit is stupid. Affliction without measure causes breakdown, not conditioning; demolition, not upbuilding; wearing away, not perfecting. Such affliction merits mockery, not congratulations. The proper measure in affliction works against indulgence, not nature, against the cause of sin, not the creation of God. . . . The proper measure is to show kindness to the body, not to serve it.

PETER OF CELLE,
ON AFFLICTION AND READING

Those who love the world neither fear nor love God, but gather to themselves all the things that please them. What they like in creatures they excuse before God, saying it was created for their use. Not fearing God, whom they should fear, they put their own will before God. Not loving God, they do not let go of their fleshly desires, nor do they rein themselves in for love of God, but with all their desire they embrace the world.

HILDEGARD OF BINGEN,
BOOK OF LIFE'S MERITS

Abstinence says: "No one should strike the lyre in such a way that its strings are damaged. But if its strings are damaged, what sound will it make? None. You, gluttony, fill up your belly so much that your veins are unhealthy. . . . I set a measure to food, so that a person neither dries up nor bloats."

HILDEGARD OF BINGEN,
BOOK OF LIFE'S MERITS

[Those who share all things in common (Acts 4.32)] rejoice because they want to be poor, not rich. Because they spurn riches as ashes that are dead because of avarice, none of them has anything according to his own will. Whatever each has through the gift of God, let her possess with God. She says that nothing is hers by her own strength, but all is from God who gives all good things to the good. And what are these? Truth and justice, which interweave with all good things.

HILDEGARD OF BINGEN,
BOOK OF LIFE'S MERITS

Greed says: "I snatch all things to myself. I hug all things to my breast; the more I have gathered the more I have. . . . When I have whatever I need, I have no worries about needing anything from someone else." Simple sufficiency replies: "You are harsh and devoid of mercy because you do not care for the advancement of others. Nothing is sufficient to satisfy you. I, however, sit above the stars, for all of God's

good things are sufficient for me. . . . Why should I desire
more than I need?"

HILDEGARD OF BINGEN,
BOOK OF LIFE'S MERITS

Because of her inner freedom, Gertrude could not bear to
keep anything that she did not need. If she received presents,
she almost always distributed them quickly to others, with
this distinction: she favored the needy, and did not prefer her
friends to her enemies. . . . In clothes and other things she
used, she always preferred what was necessary or useful to
what was unusual or pleasurable.

GERTRUDE THE GREAT,
THE HERALD OF DIVINE LOVE

O God of my life, I do not know how I may worthily praise
you or what I may give you in return, my beloved, for all the
good things that you have granted me. Consequently, I offer
you in me and me in you, my cherished Jesus, as a holocaust
of praise to you. I have nothing else. This itself, that I am
and live in you—this I give to you totally.

GERTRUDE THE GREAT,
SPIRITUAL EXERCISES

It is easy to be poor when we want nothing, to be humble
when we are despised by no one, to be patient if we never
suffer injury.

JOHN TRITHEMIUS, *RULE*

Spiritual and ascetic persons must learn to relinquish themselves and all things out of love of God. They should possess
nothing with a clinging affection of heart. They should
cling to no visible and perishable thing, to no mortal creation. They should seek the friendship, acquaintance, or
presence of no human beings, however holy, simply for the
pleasure of their company. Let them remember that not

only evil things, but even good ones, can be an impediment if they are loved and sought inordinately. . . . Never in time or in eternity should they seek something as their own. Having rejected all personal property, they should strip and deprive themselves and die to themselves and to all things.

LOUIS DE BLOIS, *SPIRITUAL DOCTRINE*

The charism of the monastic vocation is one of simplicity and truth. The monk . . . is one who abandons the routines, the clichés, the disguised idolatries and empty formalities of "the world" in order to seek the most authentic and essential meaning of the dedicated life on earth. Ideally speaking, then, the monastery should be a place of utter sincerity, without empty and deceptive formalities, without evasions, without pretenses.

THOMAS MERTON,
CONTEMPLATION IN A WORLD OF ACTION

The purpose of monastic detachment—which demands genuine sacrifice—is simply to leave the monk unencumbered, free to move, in possession of his spiritual senses and of his right mind, capable of living a charismatic life in freedom of spirit.

THOMAS MERTON,
CONTEMPLATION IN A WORLD OF ACTION

In losing touch with being and thus with God, we have fallen into a senseless idolatry of production and consumption for their own sakes. We have renounced the act of being and plunged ourself into process for its own sake.

THOMAS MERTON,
CONJECTURES OF A GUILTY BYSTANDER

Each year the new tractors get bigger and bigger, louder and louder. The one in the valley now sounds like a tank or a big bulldozer. Round and round the alfalfa field in fury. What thoughts it represents: what fury of man; what restlessness; what avidity; what desperation.

THOMAS MERTON,
CONJECTURES OF A GUILTY BYSTANDER

We do not detach ourselves from things in order to attach ourselves to God, but rather we become detached from ourselves in order to see and use all things in and for God.

THOMAS MERTON,
NEW SEEDS OF CONTEMPLATION

We are placed in this world, and it is in and through this world, not by the denial of it, that we shall come to God. But I need guidelines on this. I am surrounded by a materialistic culture and I need help in holding a balance between appreciating the material things in my life and finding myself trapped by them. Since the abbot holds the place of Christ for the community, I now translate what that means for my own self, and I then find that I am being given a most practical and immediate example of how to approach this. All the good things in my life are lent to me by Christ. They are to be cared for. Each is important and Christ has kept a list. They are on loan so that I can fulfill the assigned tasks, and they are to be collected at the end of my life, the day of judgment.

ESTHER DE WAAL, *A LIFE-GIVING WAY*

If we are foolish enough to let avarice into our hearts, it will become an insatiable tyrant.

ESTHER DE WAAL, *A LIFE-GIVING WAY*

Benedict is splendidly precise. Everything matters, down to the last detail. There is such loving and careful respect and care for clothes in the way in which they are to be washed and stored after use. There is respect for the person, too. Ill-fitting clothes are unworthy and so there is care about size and fit. . . . He picks up the theme of stewardship, and handling with a sense of responsibility.

ESTHER DE WAAL, *A LIFE-GIVING WAY*

Living in relationship with the actual place in which one finds oneself means being earthed in the immediate reality not only of time and seasons, but of the very ground itself.

ESTHER DE WAAL, *A LIFE-GIVING WAY*

Benedict wants the cellarer to be someone who knows the difference between needs and desires, who will see that the community has what is necessary but does not begin the long, slippery road into excess and creature comforts and indolence and soft-souledness.

SR. JOAN CHITTISTER,
THE RULE OF BENEDICT

Dependence on God may be what is lacking in a society where consumerism and accumulation have become the root diseases of a world in which everything is not enough and nothing satisfies.

SR. JOAN CHITTISTER,
THE RULE OF BENEDICT

Waste is not a Benedictine virtue. Planned obsolescence is not a Benedictine goal. Disposability is not a Benedictine quality. A Benedictine soul is a soul that takes care of things . . . and "treats all utensils and goods of the monastery like the sacred vessels of the altar."

SR. JOAN CHITTISTER,
THE RULE OF BENEDICT

CHAPTER 10

Discernment

Possibly no quality has been more characteristic of the monastic tradition than discernment or discretion. Even today, Benedict is praised for his discretion and Benedictines for their moderation. To profit from this tradition, it is necessary to sort out the range of meanings the term embraces. Almost all these meanings appear in the life and instructions of Saint Antony.

Antony was a veritable doctor of discernment. He was able to discern the hand of the devil in events and to distinguish which thoughts came from the devil and which from God. Antony also knew which defenses worked best against which temptations. Antony was a renowned ascetic, and according to Antony's biographer, Athanasius, he sometimes seemed ashamed of having a body, yet even in old age he remained youthful and healthy in appearance. The sayings of Antony are particularly emphatic about moderation in ascetic practices. Antony was also a man of stable character; he was not given to extremes of elation or dejection. Antony knew himself; self-knowledge is a prerequisite for discernment or a manifestation of its power.

Benedict urged moderation in food, clothing, horarium. He called discretion the mother of the virtues. Benedict's own discretion showed itself particularly in giving the strong something to strive for without discouraging the weak. Discretion identified or distinguished good and evil, both in one's own life and in the lives of others. Bede warns that those inclined to correct others should do so only if they know themselves thoroughly and have acknowledged their own faults. For Hildegard, discretion puts individuals in tune with themselves.

Discretion, then, is able to pick out the word and will of God amid all the conflicting voices emanating from the devil, from oneself, from others. The discerning, balanced person is that way partly because of natural, God-given endowment, partly through experience, and completely by grace. Experience teaches us the ways in which we fool ourselves or let ourselves be fooled. Experience teaches us when our asceticism or our self-indulgence is likely to be harmful. By discernment we know ourselves, and so humility presupposes discretion, just as discretion presupposes humility. None of this happens without experience and imagination. Through them, we learn the boundaries marked out by discretion. Discernment then is the opposite of naïveté; it is wisdom won at the risk of error.

On the next day Antony went out, inspired with an even greater zeal for the service of God. . . . He set out at once for the mountain by himself. But there was the Enemy again! Seeing his earnestness and wishing to thwart it, he projected the illusion of a large disk of silver into the road. But Antony, seeing through the trickery of the Hater of Goodness, stopped, and, looking at the disk, exposed the Devil in it, saying: "A disk in the desert. Where does that come from? This is not a well traveled highway, and there is no sign that any people have come this way. It is of great size, it could not have been dropped unnoticed. Indeed, even if it had been lost, the loser would have turned back and looked for it. He would have found it because this is desert country. This is a trick of the Devil. You will not thwart my resolution by this, Devil. Let this thing perish with you." As Antony said this, the disk disappeared like smoke leaving fire.

LIFE OF ANTONY

[Antony] spent nearly twenty years practicing the ascetic life by himself, never going out and seldom seen by others. After this, as there were many who longed and sought to imitate his holy life, some of his friends came and forcefully broke down the door and removed it. Antony came forth as out of a shrine, as one initiated into sacred mysteries and filled with the spirit of God. . . . When they saw him, they were astonished to see that his body had kept its former appearance. It was neither obese from want of exercise, nor emaciated from his fastings and struggles with the demons. He was the same man they had known before his retirement.

Again, the state of his soul was pure, for it was neither contracted by grief, nor dissipated by pleasure nor pervaded by jollity and dejection. He was not embarrassed when he saw the crowd, nor was he elated at seeing so many there to receive him. No, he had himself completely under control—a man guided by reason and stable in his character.

Through him the Lord cured many of those present who were afflicted with bodily ills, and freed others from impure spirits. He also gave Antony charm in speaking; and so he comforted many in sorrow, and others who were quarreling he turned into friends. He exhorted all to prefer nothing in the world to the love of Christ.

LIFE OF ANTONY

For all the monks who came to him, Antony had the same advice—to place their confidence in the Lord and to love him, to keep themselves from bad thoughts and pleasures of the flesh, and not to be seduced by a full stomach, as is written in Proverbs [24.15]. They should flee conceit and pray continually, sing Psalms before sleeping and after, commit to heart the commandments enjoined in the Scriptures. . . . He counseled them, "the sun must not go down, not merely on our anger [Eph 4.26], but on any other sin of ours. . . . To assure ourselves of this, it is well to hear and treasure what the Apostle says: 'Judge yourselves and prove yourselves' [2 Cor 13.5]. Wherefore, let all, daily, make an accounting of the day's and the night's activity, and if they have sinned, let them stop sinning. . . . Often we are not aware of what we are doing—we do not know it, but the Lord notices everything. Therefore, leaving judgment to Him, let us have sympathy with each other and 'bear one another's burdens' [Gal 6.2]. Ourselves let us judge; and where we fall short, let us be earnest about making up our deficiency."

LIFE OF ANTONY

This was also unique in Antony's practice of asceticism that . . . he had the gift of discerning [evil] spirits. He recognized their movements and was well aware in what direction each of them directed his effort and attack. Not only was he not fooled by them, but encouraging others who were harassed in their thoughts, he taught them how they might ward off their designs, describing the weaknesses and wiles of the spirits practicing possession. And so each went down as though anointed by him and filled with confidence against the designs of the devil and his demons.

LIFE OF ANTONY

Abba Pambo asked Abba Antony, "What should I do?" The old man told him, "Do not trust in your own righteousness, do not worry about the past, and be master of your tongue and your stomach."

ANTONY, *SAYINGS*

Antony also said, "Some have afflicted their bodies with asceticism, but they lack discernment, and so they are far from God."

ANTONY, *SAYINGS*

A hunter in the desert saw Abba Antony enjoying himself with the brothers and he was scandalized. Wanting to show him that sometimes it is necessary to take care of the needs of the brethren, the old man said to him, "Put an arrow in your bow and shoot it." So he did. The old man said, "Shoot another," and he did. Then the old man said, "Shoot yet again," and the hunter answered, "If I bend my bow too much I will break it." Then the old man said to him, "It is the same with the work of God. If we stretch the brethren beyond measure they will soon break. Sometimes it is necessary to come down to meet their needs." When he heard these words, the hunter was pierced by compunction.

ANTONY, *SAYINGS*

My beloved in the Lord—I speak to you as wise people, able to know yourselves—we know that those who know themselves know God. . . . Prepare yourselves while we have some who pray for us that the fire that Jesus came to send upon the earth [Lk 12.49] may be enkindled in your hearts, so that you may be able to exercise your heart and senses to discern the good from the bad, right from left, the eternal from the passing.

ANTONY, *LETTERS*

I want you to know, my children, that I never cease praying to God for you night and day, so that He may open the eyes of your hearts to see the principal hidden evils which the evil spirits now pour upon us daily. I ask God to give you a heart of knowledge and a spirit of discernment, so that you may be able to offer your hearts before the Father as a pure sacrifice in great holiness, without blemish.

ANTONY, *LETTERS*

Truly, my children, I want you to know that there are many who have pursued asceticism throughout their life, but lack of discernment killed them.

ANTONY, *LETTERS*

They lived a cenobitic life. So he established for them in a rule an irreproachable lifestyle and traditions profitable for their souls. These he took from the holy Scriptures: proper measure in clothing, equality in food, and decent sleeping arrangements.

LIFE OF PACHOMIUS

At another time, holy though he was, he became physically
sick. . . . Another brother, sick to death, was lying in another cell nearby. He had been ill so long his body was
mere bones. He had asked the father of the monastery to
be given a little meat, and it had not yet been given to him.
[He asked to be taken to Pachomius and repeated his request to him.] Pachomius, understanding that he deserved
what he had asked for, sighed. And when at the hour of the
brothers' meal they brought to the monk to eat exactly
what all the others had, Pachomius did not eat but said:
"Respecters of persons, where is [the precept of] the
Scripture, 'You shall love your neighbor as yourself?' Do
you not see that this man is a corpse? Why did you not take
good care of him before he made his request? And why did
you overlook him after he made it? But you will say, 'We
neglected his request because this sort of food is not customary among us.' Are there no differences among sick
persons? Are not 'all things pure to the pure' [Ti 1.15]?
And if you were unable to discern by your own judgment
that this was good, why did you not tell me?" And saying
this he wept.

LIFE OF PACHOMIUS

Once Pachomius was sailing with two other brothers in a
boat to Thomousons, and at evening, at mealtime, they
prepared [food]. As they sat down to eat, he saw the great
variety of food on the table: cheeses, figs, olives, and many
other things, and he began to eat only bread. But they indis-
criminately laid hands on everything there. One [brother]
looked up and saw him weeping. After they got up, they
queried him on the meaning of this; but he said nothing. As
they asked him a second time, he said, "It is because of you
that I am grieved, because you are not abstinent. . . . For
surely it is not a sin to eat, especially the cheap things; but it
is good not to be dominated by anything, as the Apostle says
[1 Cor 6.12]. As for me, a sinner, finding the bread good, I

was satisfied with it. Another time I will eat according to the Lord's gift.

It is a great evil not to confess one's temptation quickly to someone who has knowledge, before the evil has matured. Here is the therapy through discernment of spirits that the Lord has taught us. "If I grieve my neighbor with a word, my heart becomes contrite when convinced by the word of God, and if I do not persuade him quickly I have no rest. Unclean demons! How shall I join you apostates in a thought of blasphemy against the God who created me? I will not give in even if you should pull me to pieces in suggesting these things to me. These thoughts are not mine but yours who are going to be chastised in unquenchable fire for ever and ever. As for me, I shall not cease blessing, praising, and thanking the One who created me when I did not exist, and cursing you, for cursed indeed are you apart from the Lord." When one says these things with faith, the demon vanishes like smoke.

LIFE OF PACHOMIUS

We who have chosen this way of life must obtain perfect temperance. This is also true among seculars, but intemperance cohabits with it, because they sin with all the other senses. They gawk shamelessly and they laugh immoderately.

SYNCLETICA, SAYINGS

At all times a lack of moderation is destructive. Do not expend all your defensive weapons at one time; you will be caught unarmed and will become a prisoner in the war. Our armor is the body and our soul is the soldier; take care of both against the time of need.

LIFE OF SYNCLETICA

It is essential for us to govern our soul with all discretion, and, since we live in community, not to seek our own

interest, or to be slaves to our own will, but to obey our
spiritual mother in faith.

LIFE OF SYNCLETICA

Deny yourself in order to follow Christ. . . . Chastise the
body, do not cling to pleasures, love fasting.

RULE OF BENEDICT

Love chastity.

RULE OF BENEDICT

Beware of evil desire, because death sits at the entrance to
delight.

RULE OF BENEDICT

We think two cooked dishes are sufficient for the main daily
meal, whether it is at the sixth or ninth hour, at all times of
the year. . . . If fruit or fresh vegetables are available, let a
third dish be added. A generous pound of bread should be
enough for the day. . . . But if the work be heavy, it lies in
the power and judgment of the abbot to increase the daily
food, if that seems helpful, provided that there be no gluttony. . . . Frugality is to be maintained in all matters. All
should abstain from eating meat, except those weak from
illness.

RULE OF BENEDICT

All persons have a gift from God, one this, another that
[1 Cor 7.7], and so it is with some hesitation that we regu-
late the amount of food for others. However, taking into account the limitations of the weak, we think a *hemina* [a unit
of measure of unknown quantity] of wine per day is sufficient for each. Those to whom God gives the capacity for
abstinence should know that they will have their own reward. But if the local conditions, the work, or the summer's
heat requires more, it is up to the superior to decide, taking
care in every situation that gluttony and drunkenness do not

creep in. . . . But if local conditions are such that the measure of wine prescribed above is not obtainable, but only much less or none at all, those who live there should bless God and not murmur.

RULE OF BENEDICT

The sick who are physically weak are allowed to eat meat to restore their strength; but when their health has improved, all should abstain from meat as usual.

RULE OF BENEDICT

The abbot should arrange all things moderately, so that souls may be saved and the community may do what they do without justifiable murmuring.

RULE OF BENEDICT

All things should be done in moderation for the sake of the fainthearted.

RULE OF BENEDICT

Monastic life should always have a Lenten character, but since few are capable of that, we urge all of them together to guard the purity of their lives during these days of Lent and efface the negligences of other times during these holy days. This will happen properly if we restrain ourselves from all evil, and devote ourselves to prayer with tears, reading, compunction of heart, and abstinence.

RULE OF BENEDICT

Taking into account these and other examples of discretion, the mother of the virtues, the abbot should arrange all things so that the strong have something to strive for and the weak are not driven away.

RULE OF BENEDICT

Three days a week he ate nothing, but fasted continuously day and night. On these days he enjoined his tongue to

silence, so he would not slip in even a single word. On
the other three weekdays his food was leeks or boiled cab-
bage and a crust of bread. On Sundays, out of reverence
for the feast, he expanded his spare diet to include fish and
wine.

LIFE OF WULFSTAN

Before we correct a sinning neighbor and after we render
our neighbor the service of a deserved correction, we
should consider with a properly humble investigation
whether we ourselves are enmeshed in the very things we
condemn in him or in other crimes like his. For it often
happens, for example, that people judge a murderer who
sins publicly more harshly than the evil hatreds they fail to
recognize are despoiling them secretly, or that those who
accuse a fornicator fail to notice the plague of pride by
which they extol themselves for their chastity, or that those
who condemn a drunken person do not see the virus of
envy that consumes them.

BEDE, *HOMILIES ON THE GOSPELS*

The virtue of discretion lies dormant without the fervor of
charity; and intense fervor runs wild without the guidance
of discretion.

BERNARD OF CLAIRVAUX,
ON THE SONG OF SONGS

Zeal without knowledge is unbearable. Where there is fervent zeal, there discretion—the ordering of charity—is
most necessary. Zeal without knowledge is always less effective, less useful. Often it is found to be very harmful. Wherever zeal is most fervent and the spirit most vehement, there
the need for knowledge's oversight is all the greater. Knowledge restrains zeal, tempers the spirit, orders charity.

BERNARD OF CLAIRVAUX,
ON THE SONG OF SONGS

When the stomach hears the voice of insistent hunger, it
confuses necessity and pleasure in a deceptive tangle. It is a
rare person who can erect a wall or divider to distinguish in
his appetite between necessity and excess.

PETER OF CELLE,
THE SCHOOL OF THE CLOISTER

Rationality is surrounded by divine protection. It produces,
arranges, and distinguishes all the things that God has given.
There is nothing that it cannot subtly penetrate and discuss.

HILDEGARD OF BINGEN,
BOOK OF LIFE'S MERITS

People think they have the beauty of prudence when they
walk about in complete foolishness.

HILDEGARD OF BINGEN,
BOOK OF LIFE'S MERITS

You who wish to be sharers in the heavenly Jerusalem, praise
your creator in the sound of faith that rings through all
God's works with a praiseworthy tone of comprehending
rationality, so that from each thing it sounds praise to the
good God. Rationality is like a trumpet with a living voice
that has tasks below itself that it dispenses in creatures
through the various arts. Then the same creatures can assist
it by returning a good, strong sound. Rationality through
the sound of its living voice makes those things that do not
have living sound resound with reason. From the first breath
by which God breathes it into the human soul, it has a jubilant mode. Therefore, praise God in that pure and fitting
knowledge that makes the creature in tune with itself, and in
the gentle and deep wisdom that arranges all things wisely in
a just dispensation—namely, when it discerns heavenly matters wisely in the minds of human beings and senses earthly
matters smoothly. For the human soul has harmony within
it and is symphonic.

HILDEGARD OF BINGEN,
BOOK OF LIFE'S MERITS

Benedict was a closed fountain [Song 4.12] who poured forth his doctrine in the discretion of God. For he drove in the sharp nail [spigot] of his doctrine neither too high nor too low, but in the middle of the wheel, so that each one, whether strong or weak or sick, would be able to drink according to his capacity.

HILDEGARD OF BINGEN,
EXPLANATION OF THE RULE OF BENEDICT

Superiors, for the love of God do not burden human weakness with more new ceremonies and observances than it can bear. Remember the warning of our holy Father in the *Rule:* ponder and temper the works you enjoin, remembering the discretion of Holy Jacob, who said: "If I drive my flocks too much, they will die in a single day." Therefore, so moderate everything that the strong have something to strive for and the weak are not forced to flee [cf. *Rule of Benedict* 64.20]. See, then, beloved fathers, how pleasing discretion is to God.

LUDOVICO BARBO, *LETTERS*

It is better to do good by abstinence than to eat without sinning.

JOHN TRITHEMIUS, *RULE*

One should not heedlessly embrace unusual austerity. Genuine love of God joins a person much more closely to God, and more quickly and effectively restrains and conquers the wantonness of the flesh. God customarily exercises and burdens those who fully resign themselves to him and are prepared to accept any troubles from his hand and to bear them patiently as long as it pleases him. Dedicated persons should therefore not oppress their bodies with excessive abstinence, vigils, and austerities of their own choosing, nor should they treat them too gently. Instead, let them observe the moderation of holy discretion in all things and accept the sane advice of others.

LOUIS DE BLOIS, *SPIRITUAL DOCTRINE*

In refreshing the body with food, drink, or sleep, one should aim at sustaining nature, not at pleasure. One should take each morsel of food and each swallow of drink with moderation and self-control, with holy fear and self-mortification for the glory of God. . . . One should seek simple rather than sumptuous things for one's use. Do not seek superfluous things, but prefer want to abundance.

> LOUIS DE BLOIS, *SPIRITUAL DOCTRINE*

Authentic renewal is going to demand a great deal of variety and originality in experimentation.

> THOMAS MERTON,
> *CONTEMPLATION IN A WORLD OF ACTION*

One cannot simply open his eyes and see. The work of understanding involves not only dialectic, but a long labor of acceptance, obedience, liberty, and love.

> THOMAS MERTON,
> *CONJECTURES OF A GUILTY BYSTANDER*

As the seasons change and the nights grow shorter, Benedict chooses to shorten the time of prayer rather than the time of sleep.

> ESTHER DE WAAL, *A LIFE-GIVING WAY*

The key word is moderation. Just as the brothers are to have sufficient, not superfluous goods. . . so also the cellarer is to steer a mid-point between being either extravagant or mean. It is waste in particular that Benedict warns against.

> ESTHER DE WAAL, *A LIFE-GIVING WAY*

[Benedict's concern regarding food] is not simply about having sufficient food, enough but not superfluous, but about the right handling of these good things. That is why there is a choice of dishes, so that all can expect to eat with enjoyment. That is why when there are fruits and fresh vegetables in season, they are to be added to the table. That is why he is not mean with the bread allowance. To look forward to a meal because it is carefully chosen and carefully presented gives to every meal something of a sacramental quality.

ESTHER DE WAAL, *A LIFE-GIVING WAY*

The purpose of fasting is simply to center on God. The discipline of fasting will reveal to me more than any other discipline what really controls me. It is no longer possible to cover up my interior dependencies—food, good things, praise, anger, envy. Fasting, therefore, plays its part in the movement of freedom, of dissociation and non-possession.

ESTHER DE WAAL, *A LIFE-GIVING WAY*

CHAPTER 11

Peace

The nineteenth-century refounders of Benedictine monasticism mistakenly selected "Ora et Labora" (Work and Pray) as their motto. A more venerable and accurate motto would be "Pax," the Latin word for "peace." Monasticism is a many-sided effort at peace, within the individual monk, between monks, between the monastery and the surrounding communities, and ultimately in the whole of church and society. We have learned enough from Gandhi and the civil rights movement to know that peace is not a ploy of the weak, but an achievement of the strong and the courageous.

Beginning with Antony and the desert monks and nuns, a favorite symbol of monastic peace was the harmony monastics established with wild animals. Antony made peace with the wild animals who disturbed his garden, Benedict was served by crows, and in Switzerland, the Irish monk Saint Gall established good relations with a bear. The lamb and lion lay down together as the desert or the wilderness was transformed into a new Eden.

Not only was Antony at peace with the world of nature and with the people around him; he was at peace with himself. He radiated a peace and joy that attracted strangers to him. The inner peace of his heart was somehow etched on his face.

Good monastic leaders are able to maintain peace within their communities. Pachomius, who seems to have been a brilliant leader of men, worked hard to develop a potential successor. In the end, his efforts were partially foiled, and we hear the author of his biography lamenting the loss of the peace that the communities enjoyed during his lifetime.

Peace was an important concept for Saint Benedict, in part because of this earlier monastic tradition. Peace also figured prominently in the Bible, where it was a state of earthly plenty and of harmony with God, people, and nature. Biblical peace is God's gift, but also a central goal of human effort. For Saint Augustine and the classical Christian writers of the centuries before Benedict, peace was the tranquillity of order, based on observance of the laws God established for the world he created.

In the prologue of the *Rule of Benedict* Jesus is quoted using the words of a psalm (Ps 33.16) to tell those who desire life to seek peace and pursue it. Benedict wanted his monks to make peace with each other before sundown, and several times the *Rule* warns against making a feigned or insincere peace. He designed his rules on the distribution of goods so that "all the members of the family shall be at peace." Guests are to be given the sign of peace when they arrive, just as if they were Christ. Benedict's rules on rank in the community are for the sake of peace.

Read in the light of its biblical and classical background, Benedict's most basic requirement for peace is the tranquillity of order based on the observance of the laws of nature—for example, getting enough sleep, avoiding workaholism, taking care of the sick. Second, there should be a harmony between being, thought, word, and action; for example, an abbot should be what he is called, the mind should be in harmony with the voice. Third, the atmosphere of the monastery should be quiet and orderly, so that those who are there may also be at peace. Peace of soul means avoiding worry, excessive needs and wants, inflexibility, envy. Peace of soul presupposes that we seek to be content with life as we find it. To do that we must learn to control our desires, develop equanimity of character, and achieve unity with God. That is a lifetime's work—the summit of virtue, Benedict calls it. Even so, any peace on earth will be partial and fragile; lasting and perfect peace is for heaven.

The monastic enterprise is to create people and communities of peace, so it is not surprising that authors indicate that peace presupposes almost every other activity and virtue mentioned in this book. Peace can be achieved only where conflict is honestly acknowledged. To acknowledge such conflict takes courage and humility and an uncommon readiness to forgive. To honesty, courage, humility, and forgiveness must be added workable mechanisms of conflict resolution. Genuine peace is not easily or painlessly achieved. However, the alternative is open conflict, or worse yet, a false peace, a facade of order fronting a house at odds with itself.

At first, wild animals in the desert coming for water often would damage the beds of Antony's garden. But he caught one of the animals, held it gently, and said to them all: "Why do you do harm to me when I harm none of you? Go away, and in the Lord's name do not come near these things again!" And ever afterwards, as though awed by his orders, they did not come near the place.

LIFE OF ANTONY

[Antony's face] had a great and indescribable charm in it. And he had this added gift from the Savior: if he was present in a gathering of monks and someone who had no previous acquaintance with him wished to see him, as soon as he arrived he would pass over the others and run to Antony as if drawn by his eyes. It was not his stature or figure that made him stand out from the rest, but his settled character and the purity of his soul. For his soul was not perturbed, and so his outward appearance was calm. The joy in his soul expressed itself in the cheerfulness of his face.

LIFE OF ANTONY

Now it is not yet five years since he [Pachomius] passed away and we have forgotten that very great joy and peace which we then had with each other. For in the days of our father, we did not have either in heart or in mouth anything but the word of God which is sweeter than honey and the honeycomb [Ps 19.10]. We were not conscious of living on earth but of feasting in heaven.

LIFE OF PACHOMIUS

Hate no one. Do not be jealous. Do not act out of envy. Do
not love quarreling.

RULE OF BENEDICT

If there is discord, make peace before the sun goes down.

RULE OF BENEDICT

Wulfstan spent much of the day in preaching. He tried to
inculcate in his hearers that which he knew they needed
most—peace. For mortal men can hear of nothing sweeter,
seek nothing more desirable, find nothing better. Peace is
the beginning and the end of human salvation, the ultimate
goal of God's commands. The angelic music sang of it at the
first sign of our redemption, the Lord gave it to his disciples
when he had foreseen the impending Crucifixion, and at the
Resurrection restored it to them as a trophy of victory.

LIFE OF WULFSTAN

"What then will you give us, Lord? What are you going to
give us?" "Peace I give you. My peace I leave for you," says
the Lord. That is enough for me: gratefully I accept what
you leave, and I let go of what you retain. If it pleases you,
I do not doubt that it is for my good. . . . I want peace, I desire peace, and nothing more. If there is anyone unsatisfied
with peace, they will be unsatisfied with you.

BERNARD OF CLAIRVAUX,
ON THE SONG OF SONGS

In you, O Jesus, true peace, may I have peace upon peace
forever, so that through you I may come to that peace which
surpasses all understanding, where happily I may see you in
yourself forever. Amen.

GERTRUDE THE GREAT,
SPIRITUAL EXERCISES

I urge you, above all, if you want to obtain the true fruit
of prayers, strive to be in charity and peace with all by

forgiving those who offend you, by loving the virtuous, by serving all with humility, and by obeying your superiors in all things with a ready will, so that true peace may arise in your minds, and our Lord God, whose place is the peace in our minds, may reside in a peaceful place. I am confident in saying that in a short time you will reach these virtues and this peace through the use of [vocal] prayer.

LUDOVICO BARBO, *FORM OF PRAYER*

Humility is at the service of peace and concord.

JOHN TRITHEMIUS, *RULE*

There is nothing good where there is no peace. God is a lover of peace and dwells only in peaceful hearts. No matter what one has, it gives no joy if peace is lacking.

JOHN TRITHEMIUS, *RULE*

If you want to keep peace in the community, judge yourself and no one else. Be careful never to disturb the peace of your brothers, for whoever destroys the peace of just people makes himself a persecutor of God.

JOHN TRITHEMIUS, *RULE*

Blessed are those to whom Jesus speaks inwardly, saying, "Come up to a desert place." Blessed, I say, are those whom the Lord carries across the great, wide sea through countless dangers of this world to the port of monastic life. There life is truly quiet and secure; there tranquillity, peace, and spiritual joy abound; there, day and night, holy people freely serve the king of the ages without care or concern about passing things. They have only one concern, that they may please their great God through a firm commitment to obedience, through pleasant devotion in prayer, through sweet exercises of holy reading, through gentle baptism in holy tears.

LOUIS DE BLOIS, *MIRROR FOR MONKS*

Father, I beg you to keep me in this silence so that I may learn from it the word of your peace and the word of your mercy and the word of your gentleness to the world: and that through me perhaps your word of peace may make itself heard where it has not been possible for anyone to hear it for a long time.

THOMAS MERTON,
CONJECTURES OF A GUILTY BYSTANDER

[The cellarer] is indeed a model of non-violence, and the very way in which he handles people demonstrates a profound spiritual truth: people are to be handled with respect and reverence. But the cellarer is to handle himself with gentleness. He is to show these same qualities toward himself in the way in which he takes care of his own body and spirit. . . . The cellarer is not too proud to admit that he may need help. He is prepared to delegate, not seeing himself as indispensable. He knows the importance of drawing lines so that he is not endlessly accessible. He makes himself available at established times. . . . Handling with care applies just as much to my own self as it does to other people and to the material world. . . . And the purpose? So that he remain calm. Peace is fundamental in the Rule.

ESTHER DE WAAL, A LIFE-GIVING WAY

Benedictinism simply sets out to gentle a universe riddled with violence by being a peaceful voice for peace in a world that thinks that everything . . . is accomplished by force.

SR. JOAN CHITTISTER,
THE RULE OF BENEDICT

[Benedict extended the use of Alleluia in the liturgy of the hours to every day of the year except during Lent.] The prescription is a telling one. To the Benedictine mind, life in all its long nights and weary days is something to be praised, death is the rivet of joy, there is no end to the positive. Even

life in hot fields and drab offices and small houses is somehow one long happy thought when God is its center, and
blessings, however rare, however scant, are blessed.

SR. JOAN CHITTISTER,
THE RULE OF BENEDICT

CHAPTER 12

Patience

Patience comes from the Latin verb *pati,* which means "to suffer, to undergo, to endure." Gertrude's fanciful etymology of *pax* plus *scientia* (knowledge) is correct to the extent that knowing the purpose of suffering goes a long way toward making suffering bearable. Syncletica suggests that if monastics think they are burdened with much suffering, they should think about the burdens of their married sisters out beyond the protection of the cloister walls.

The Christian monastic tradition connects patience with Christ's sufferings, his "passion," another derivative of *pati.* A telling example is Benedict's statement in the prologue to his *Rule:* "We will share by patience in the sufferings of Christ, so that we may deserve to be sharers in his kingdom" (*Rule of Benedict* prologue 50). Christian efforts to understand suffering inevitably lead to the paschal mystery, the dying and rising of Christ, the seed that must die if it is to bear fruit. Hence suffering can coexist with joy, not because suffering is either unreal or invariably mild, but because it is a path to life.

Patience is essential, since the road to virtue is a long one. Only repeated effort and practice establish a habit, and a firm habit is frequently exercised. Especially at the beginning, the road is difficult. Amma Syncletica's comparison with lighting a fire mirrors the reality nicely.

There are some injustices we must accept since they are unavoidable. Others we might protest, but shouldn't, because the disruptive effects of such a protest outweigh any good effects it might achieve. In some cases we are obligated to protest. In all but the last case, one should bear persecution for justice's sake. Such patience is a gift, rooted in the faith that God is in charge of the universe, and that

God's Providence can and will bring good out of bad. As a friend reminded me recently, suffering entered into willingly leads us to the will of God, which may not be what we wanted or hoped for. Accepting annoyances and suffering as special gifts of God who loves us to perfection may take us out of ourselves and show us, in other people, the face of Christ turned toward us.

Perhaps the most difficult exercise of patience is to maintain it with our own failings. Our struggle to practice virtue often takes place on the verge of defeat, or it consists of trying to get back on our feet after falling yet again. God is patient with us, so we can afford to be patient also. Esther de Waal makes the wise observation that the *Rule* provides for the complete range of human weakness, but is neither cynical nor pessimistic. This patience of the *Rule* reflects the patience of God. We are saved not by our perfection, but by our identification with the dying and rising of Christ.

An old man said: "If you become sick from a bodily illness, don't lose courage. If your Lord wishes to afflict your body, why should you be upset? Does not his concern for you include everything? Can you live without him? Be patient then and pray that he will give you what you should have. His will is that you stay in your room with patience and that you eat what is given to you as alms."

SAYINGS OF THE DESERT
FATHERS AND MOTHERS

A brother, irritated with another, prayed, asking to be patient toward this brother. He prayed that the temptation would pass without causing him any harm. Immediately he saw smoke leave his mouth.

SAYINGS OF THE DESERT
FATHERS AND MOTHERS

Let us women not be misled by the thought that those in the world are without cares. For perhaps in comparison they struggle more than we do. For towards women generally there is great hostility in the world. They bear children with difficulty and risk, and they suffer patiently through nursing, and they share illnesses with their sick children—and these things they endure without having any limit to their travail. For either the children they bear are maimed in body, or, brought up in perversity, they treacherously murder their parents. Since we women know these facts, therefore, let us not be deluded by the Enemy that their life is easy and care-free. For in giving birth women die in labor, and yet, in failing to give birth, they waste away under reproaches that they are barren and unfruitful.

LIFE OF SYNCLETICA

For those who are making their way to God there is at first great struggle and effort, but then indescribable joy. For just as those who wish to kindle a fire are at first choked with smoke, suffer watery eyes, and in this way achieve their purpose (indeed Scripture says: "Our God is a consuming fire" [Heb 12.29]), so we too must kindle the divine fire within us with tears and effort.

LIFE OF SYNCLETICA

Let us also understand this profitable thing we heard from our father [Theodore], from his interpretations of the holy Scriptures, about a man wishing to be purified from a sin such as anger. Unless he says in himself when he is reviled the first time, "Behold, today I have gained a golden coin," and unless he considers it a further gain when he is reviled a second time, and so on until he has an abundance of gold, it is impossible for him not to get angry. . . . Such are the men of God. Not only did they bear those who persecuted them and did them evil, but they even prayed for them, according to the commandment of the Savior, whose gold they were going to inherit according to the Scripture, "Heirs of God, and coheirs with Christ" [Rom 8.17].

LIFE OF PACHOMIUS

Bear persecution for the sake of justice.

RULE OF BENEDICT

Those who show patience in adversities and injustices fulfill the command of the Lord that says: "Those who are struck on one cheek should offer the other" [Mt 5.39].

RULE OF BENEDICT

Never departing from his instruction, but persevering in his teaching in the monastery until death, we will share by patience in the sufferings of Christ, so that we may deserve to be sharers in his kingdom.

RULE OF BENEDICT

[We ought] to be of help to all; to refrain from hurting others out of bitterness, to bear whatever injuries are inflicted on us, and even ask pardon from the Lord for those who inflict them.

BEDE, *HOMILIES ON THE GOSPELS*

People who are committed to praying frequently have experienced what I am talking about. Often we approach the altar with a lukewarm and arid heart in order to devote ourselves to prayer. If we are persistent, our heart is suddenly filled with grace.

BERNARD OF CLAIRVAUX,
ON THE SONG OF SONGS

Heavenly joy declares: I give all my works to God, because in some sadness there is joy, and in some pleasure there is no prosperity.

HILDEGARD OF BINGEN,
BOOK OF LIFE'S MERITS

[Gertrude] firmly believed that everything, external or internal, worked together for her good.

GERTRUDE THE GREAT,
THE HERALD OF DIVINE LOVE

The Lord told M[echthild] in prayer: "The *patientia* (patience) that I like in Gertrude comes from the words *pax* (peace) and *scientia* (knowledge). The fervor of her patience should be such that in adversity she does not lose her peace of heart, but always strives to think why she is suffering—namely, out of love as a sign of true faithfulness.

GERTRUDE THE GREAT,
THE HERALD OF DIVINE LOVE

Christ says: "Deny yourself, so that you can follow me," and "Take up your cross daily" [Mk 8.34]. Those who patiently and freely suffer all adversities for God take up their cross daily. Our cross consists of the difficult obstacles of this life through which we travel to God. "Take up,"—that is, bear them cheerfully and willingly. "Take up your cross and follow me." It is of no use to deny ourselves and bear the cross unless we also follow Christ.

JOHN TRITHEMIUS, *RULE*

For all the living, life is the most desirable thing. We all want to live and reign with Christ, but we do not all want to suffer with Christ.

JOHN TRITHEMIUS, *RULE*

Nothing is hard for the advanced person or for the one who loves or is perfect. But for beginners, even easy things are hard, for they invite the mind spiritually to acts that are contrary to its usual way of acting.

JOHN TRITHEMIUS, *RULE*

Whatever happens to them, let them refer it to the divine will and accept it just as it comes from the hand of God, without whose Providence not even a leaf falls from a tree to the earth. . . . Let them bear with patient and tranquil minds internal abandonment and disaster as well as any afflictions, and let them praise God, believing that he is willing and able to promote their salvation in all circumstances.

LOUIS DE BLOIS, *SPIRITUAL DOCTRINE*

Persist in your holy purpose, even if you fail a thousand
times a day.

LOUIS DE BLOIS, *SPIRITUAL MIRROR*

When you are afflicted with sensory distractions, depres-
sion, dryness of heart, headache, or any other misery and
temptation, beware of saying: "I am abandoned. The Lord
has cast me off. My service does not please him." These are
things that the faint-hearted often say. Instead, bear all
things patiently and cheerfully for the sake of him who
called and chose you. Believe for certain that he is near to
those who are troubled in heart.

LOUIS DE BLOIS, *MIRROR FOR MONKS*

Benedict is always showing me the patience of God waiting
and working for the return of his children. Throughout the
prologue, he never fails to situate our lives in the context of
this patience of God which is no less than the paschal mystery working in us through the *patientia,* the suffering of
Christ.

ESTHER DE WAAL, *A LIFE-GIVING WAY*

What I have increasingly appreciated as I have stayed with
the Rule is finding how it provides for the whole range of
human weakness and inadequacy, yet with a complete absence of cynicism or pessimism. This is what the human
condition is, and this is where God's grace is encountered
and the paschal mystery happens. . . . Benedict would seem
to be saying that weakness and failure are not necessarily a
handicap or a disqualification but can, with help, be made
the place in which the power of the crucified and risen
Christ can be manifested in our lives.

ESTHER DE WAAL, *A LIFE-GIVING WAY*

CHAPTER 13

Separation

Monasticism is by definition a countercultural movement, not because monastics make it a point to define themselves against any existing culture, but because they try to maintain their own values and virtues, whatever values the surrounding culture may exhibit. At their best and wisest, monastics listen to and learn from existing culture, but they do so critically, with a preexisting understanding of who they are and who they want to be.

To maintain monastic culture, monks limit their contact with the surrounding culture by means of cloister or separation from the world. In part, cloister is spatial; a wall beyond which the monk usually does not go except for brief and necessary forays. More essentially, cloister is a matter of mind and heart. Monastics monitor what they read, watch, and hear, and learn to make sure that they can hear God's voice and that the Biblical tradition pulses as the heart of their community.

Peter of Celle may be somewhat sanguine about the correlation between staying in a cloister and stretching the mind. However, the mind that withdraws from gossip, useless news, potboiler novels, and surfing the Internet will have much more time and energy for God, and for praying, reading, thinking, and listening to and caring for other people—activities that do stretch the mind. The monastic writers spoke of dispersal and collection. People serious about living deeply should gather the rubble of their lives and glue themselves back together.

It is one thing to love one's room because one is so stressed out by work, crowds, talking, rushing from one appointment to the next, answering phone messages, that one's room is a place where one can collapse in peace. It is another thing to find somewhere a place of silence and creativity, where one can listen for the voice of God and think one's own thoughts and be one's own self.

Once when Antony had been importuned by people who needed assistance and the military commander had sent numerous messengers asking him to come down, he came and spoke a few words on the subject of salvation and in behalf of those who wanted him, and then hastened to leave. When the duke, as he is called, begged him to stay, he said he could not spend any time with them, and satisfied him by a beautiful comparison: "Just as fish exposed for any length of time on dry land die, so monks go to pieces when they loiter among you and spend too much time with you. Therefore, we must be off to the mountain, as fish to the sea. Otherwise, if we tarry, we may lose sight of the inner life."

LIFE OF ANTONY

Abba Antony said that a time is coming when men will go mad, a time when, if they will see someone who is not mad, they will attack him saying, "You are mad, because you are not like us."

ANTONY, *SAYINGS*

Abba Antony once went to visit Abba Amoun in Mount Nitria. During their visit Abba Amoun said, "Since by your prayers the number of the brethren increases, some of them want to build their cells at a distance where they may live in peace. How far away from here do you think we should build their cells?" Abba Antony said, "We will eat at the ninth hour and then go for a walk in the desert and explore the country." So they went out into the desert and walked until sunset. Then Abba Antony said, "Let us pray and plant the cross here, so that those who wish to do so may build here. Then when those who remain behind want to visit those who have come here, they can come after taking a little food at the ninth hour. If they do this, they will be able to keep in touch with each other without distraction." The distance is twelve miles.

ANTONY, *SAYINGS*

Not all courses are suitable for all people. You should have confidence in your own disposition. For many it is profitable to live in community; for others it is helpful to withdraw on their own. . . . Many people have found salvation in a city while imagining the conditions of a desert. And many though on a mountain, have been lost by living the life of townspeople. It is possible for one who is in a group to be alone in thought, and for one who is alone to live mentally with a crowd.

LIFE OF SYNCLETICA

We have committed ourselves to exile, that is, we are outside secular boundaries; we have, then, been banished— let us not seek the same ends.

LIFE OF SYNCLETICA

Make yourself a stranger to the world's activities.

RULE OF BENEDICT

Keep death daily before your eyes.

RULE OF BENEDICT

If possible, the monastery should be located so that all necessities—that is, water, mill, garden, and various crafts— are provided within the monastery, so that there will be no need for monks to wander forth, which is not good for their souls.

RULE OF BENEDICT

Those who are about to set out on a journey should commend themselves to the prayer of the community and abbot. . . . Nor should they presume to tell anyone else what they saw or heard outside the monastery, because this has caused great harm.

RULE OF BENEDICT

It feels good to rest after working. After having been troubled all year with painful and unrelenting problems, I am thirsting mightily for the modest silence of my room as a desirable haven. I draw deeply from the silence now granted. My mind finds a more expansive rest by being within these four walls than by traveling around outside to the four corners of the earth. In fact, the smaller the place, the more the mind stretches, for when the body is held in check, the mind rises up; curbing the body brings expansion of the mind.

PETER OF CELLE,
ON AFFLICTION AND READING

[Staying quietly in one's room] is not among those pleasures that I find cloying once they are attained though they were desirable before being possessed. A room is experienced in two ways, depending on the lifestyle of the person who lives in it. To carnal people it is a harsh environment, to spiritual people a pleasant one. It is a prison to the flesh, a paradise for the mind.

PETER OF CELLE,
ON AFFLICTION AND READING

The need for a certain distance from the world does not make the monk love the world less. Nor does it imply that he never has any contact with the outside world. Certainly the monastic community has the right and duty to create a certain solitude for the monks: it is no sin to live a silent life. But at the same time the mo-

nastic community owes other men a share in that quiet and
that solitude.

THOMAS MERTON,
CONTEMPLATION IN A WORLD OF ACTION

[Speaking of his affinity for Albert Camus, Merton says it is
easy for him to take Camus's position:] that of a man who at
once loves the world yet stands apart from it with a critical
objectivity which refuses to become involved in its transient
fashions and its more manifest absurdities.

THOMAS MERTON,
CONTEMPLATION IN A WORLD OF ACTION

The monk is by definition a man who lives in seclusion, in
solitude, in silence outside of the noise and the confusion of
a busy worldly existence. He does this because seclusion
provides certain necessary conditions for his life: an interior
freedom, silence, liberation from trivial concerns that arise
from the overstimulation of the appetites and the imagination. The monk finally seeks solitude and silence, let us admit it, because he knows that the real fruit of his vocation is
union with God in love and contemplation.

THOMAS MERTON,
CONTEMPLATION IN A WORLD OF ACTION

In Louisville, at the corner of Fourth and Walnut, in the
center of the shopping district, I was suddenly overwhelmed
with the realization that I love all those people, that they
were mine and I theirs, that we could not be alien to one
another even though we were total strangers. It was like
waking from a dream of separateness, of spurious self-
isolation in a special world. . . . Though "out of the world"
we are in the same world as everybody else, the world of the
bomb, the world of race hatred, the world of technology,
the world of mass media, big business, revolution, and all
the rest. . . . It is a glorious destiny to be a member of the

human race, though it is a race dedicated to many absurdities and one which makes many terrible mistakes: yet, with all that, God Himself gloried in becoming a member of the human race.

THOMAS MERTON,
CONJECTURES OF A GUILTY BYSTANDER

Benedictine spirituality goes into the heart in order to embrace the world. It forms us differently than the world forms us but it does not attempt to shape us independently of the real world around us.

SR. JOAN CHITTISTER,
THE RULE OF BENEDICT

CHAPTER 14

Stability

A healthy human life is a combination of fidelity to commitments on the one hand, and growth, change, and development on the other. One thinks of the Israelites, who made their covenant with God, then entered the promised land, took up settled agriculture, and developed structures of government and cohesion. Or of Ruth, who, having committed herself to Naomi with the promise "I will go where you go," did so, met Boaz, married, and started life afresh. Jesus himself was fundamentally committed to doing his father's will. For thirty years this kept him in Nazareth, probably working at his father's trade, learning it better, and growing in grace and wisdom. Then when he was almost thirty Jesus came to see that his fidelity to God's will for him required a radical change in his life, a change that involved a year or two as a wandering preacher, and then a momentous journey to Jerusalem, where he was tortured and executed, and rose again.

The *Rule of Benedict* endorses fidelity and change by the two vows of stability and conversion. Stability commits one to a certain community and its way of life; conversion calls one to continuously grow and follow the lead of God's will as this appears in one's deepest desires, in one's circumstances, and in the advice and authority of other people (listening and obedience). There is clearly a tension here, one that can be resolved only in dialogue, prayer, and love: in dialogue, to help the individual and community discern; in prayer, because it is God's will they are seeking; in love, because love is an unselfish and caring affirmation of the being and goodness of another. The tension is less when communities that value and respect the gifts and callings of individuals try to give them scope for growth and change. The same tension between fidelity and change occurs in almost every significant human relationship.

The vow of stability attaches the monk to a single community or monastery. There is very little that ties one Benedictine monastery to another. Almost all are in congregations of monasteries that provide member communities with regular visitations, meetings, and support but leave the individual monasteries autonomous. The advantage of this is that the monk has to learn to live with and for the community he has chosen. He cannot just move from place to place as he becomes discouraged with one community and then another. He has to face the situation and learn the truth about himself and the human condition. A disadvantage is that the monk is very deeply defined by his community; any dysfunction in that community will affect him either directly or indirectly.

For the most part, monasteries are not in the vanguard of change. They may call into question the certitudes of the dominant culture, but they are slow to change their own ways of doing things. For one thing, most of the customary ways of doing things are in place precisely so that the monks do not have to think about them. One knows when to eat lunch, where to sit, whether to talk, what prayers to say, and so one can concentrate on doing them well rather than think about what to do next. These customary ways of doing things are second nature, a second nature defined in part by the requirements of community living, in part by the values monks espouse. That is why Ludovico Barbo, for one, says that customary observances should not be changed readily.

However, conservatism in monastic customs may gradually turn to fossilization. Monastic education, monastic work and economy, monastic organization, and monastic recruitment are all in great flux today. These and other issues call for imagination and experimentation. One needs to decide what is the best possible course of action and then do it, leaving the results in God's hands. Stability must provide a ground for innovation, for continual renewal of *conversatio*. Barbo was an example of such innovation in his time.

Here, too, discernment is the key. The monastic vows aim at a subtle combination of stability and openness to change. Innovation on a foundation of stability, and firm commitment in the midst of renewal or innovation, are not easy. They seem to be the principal challenge of our time. Hence, we probably should be kinder to those who seem out of tune with the rest of us; they may be in tune with the future.

Similarly, as Bede points out, discernment helps us to know ourselves and to perceive where we need to grow in virtue and integrity. The acquisition of virtue is the moral equivalent of physical stability. One becomes morally stable by acquiring virtue. The Benedictine tradition suggests that a certain stability of place and lifestyle is an advantageous setting for moral growth and stability.

Someone asked Abba Antony, "What should I do in order to please God?" The old man answered: "Pay attention to what I am going to tell you: wherever you go, always have God before your eyes; do everything you do according to the testimony of the holy Scriptures; wherever you live, do not leave it easily."

ANTONY, *SAYINGS*

An old man said: "The fathers did not leave the place where they were except for one of three causes: if there was someone there who was angry with them and they were unable to win him over; if they were praised too much; or if they risked falling into temptation."

SAYINGS OF THE DESERT
FATHERS AND MOTHERS

A brother asked one of the old men: "What should I do? My thoughts torment me, saying: 'You can neither keep a fast nor work; at least go and visit the sick, for that is a work of charity.'" The old man told him: "Go, eat, drink, sleep, only don't leave your cell. Know that perseverance in his room keeps the monk in his regular routine." When he has passed some days, he became bored, and, finding some small branches of palm, he split them; then the next day he wove them. After having worked, he said: "There are still some other small branches that I will prepare before I eat." He prepared them; then he said: "I will go read a little, then I will eat." After having read, he said: "I will recite my brief psalmody, then I will eat quietly." Thus he progressed little by little with the help of God until he restored his regular routine. In acting confidently against his tormenting thoughts, he conquered them.

SAYINGS OF THE DESERT
FATHERS AND MOTHERS

Do you live in a cenobitic monastery? Do not change your location, for you will be greatly harmed. For just as a bird that abandons its eggs renders them empty and unfruitful, so a nun or a monk grows cold and dies to faith by moving from place to place.

LIFE OF SYNCLETICA

We must follow in [the] footsteps [of our predecessors in the faith] in our own time, my brothers, directing the ordering of our life according to the example of good people and persisting until death in our commitment to an upright life.

BEDE, HOMILIES ON THE GOSPELS

By digging deeply they alertly examine their consciences so that nothing sordid may lie hidden within them. They carefully probe all the depths of their hearts for the hiding places of empty thoughts and draw them out with the hand of conscientious discretion so that they can prepare a firm and restful throne within themselves for that strong rock, who is Christ. And through his presence they persevere amid the fearful adversities of this world and amid its allurements as well.

BEDE, HOMILIES ON THE GOSPELS

Albero, a man of noteworthy virtue and age, skilled in book decoration, saw something at the time of calamity and anguish when the father [Abbot Hugh] died that deserves mention. It happened that a certain uncle of his had chosen him to be his companion on a pilgrimage to Compostela. But when he came to the gate, blessed Hugh met him with a serene and angelic face and chided him with the words: "Where are you going, Albero? Stay! Why are you going away?" Albero said to him: "How can I remain here when I do not find you here anymore, you who were sent here as a tower of David, a column, a wall for the upright of Israel. Like a sheep without a shepherd wanders a monk deprived of his abbot." The abbot, whom Albero saw in his spirit's imagination, replied: "Those whom God raises in heaven are not taken down from their assigned place. Those who stay in their rightful place in this world receive a higher place above."

LIFE OF HUGH OF CLUNY

When you are feeling strong, do not be complacent, but call to God with the prophet and say: "When my strength fails me, do not abandon me" [Ps 70.9]. And in time of temptation be consoled and say with the bride: "Draw me after you, and we shall run in the odor of your ointments" [Ps 33.2]. Thus you will not lose hope in bad times, nor will foresight desert you in good times, and amid both the prosperity and adversity of changing times you will retain a certain image of eternity—that is, this inviolable and unshakable constancy of a stable soul—blessing the Lord at every moment. In this way you claim for yourself, even amid the doubtful events and inevitable deficiencies of this changing world, a certain status of lasting unchangeability while you begin to renew and reform yourself according to the ancient pattern of likeness to the eternal God, "in whom there is neither alteration nor the shadow of change" [Jas 1.17].

BERNARD OF CLAIRVAUX,
ON THE SONG OF SONGS

People who wish to dispel from themselves the wicked spirits who urge them to be constantly changing and desire to flee their punishments should, if they be laypeople, collect themselves to lead a spiritual life, and if they be claustrals, let them confine themselves more strictly than usual in their way of life with all the discipline that truth requires, so that they can cast off the wickedness of this vice.

HILDEGARD OF BINGEN,
BOOK OF LIFE'S MERITS

Our conversion is pleasing to God when we persevere to the end and complete the good that we have begun.

JOHN TRITHEMIUS, *RULE*

[To people outside of a monastic community, the three Benedictine vows of stability, obedience, and conversion of life appear to be] three promises that together form one whole process. They ask me to enter into a dynamic commitment that simultaneously holds me still (stability) and moves me forward (continual conversion) with all the time God, and not my own self, as the point of reference (obedience, listening intently).

ESTHER DE WAAL, *A LIFE-GIVING WAY*

In the end I am brought back, of course, to Christ himself and to his example, the willingness to endure faithfully and with patience, *patientia,* reminding me that this means both waiting and suffering. What makes this possible? The faithfulness of God. God is faithful to the covenant, and I know I can rely on him. . . . My stability is possible in the end because of the certain, guaranteed, steadfastness of God.

ESTHER DE WAAL, *A LIFE-GIVING WAY*

It is not perfection that leads us to God; it is perseverance.

SR. JOAN CHITTISTER,
THE RULE OF BENEDICT

No one . . . has a call simply to a particular place, as good as it may be. The call of God is to the Will of God. Consequently, though every institution mediates the call of God for us, every vocation transcends any particular institution.

SR. JOAN CHITTISTER,
THE RULE OF BENEDICT

CHAPTER 15

Obedience

Obedience *(ob-audire)* is related to listening *(audire)*. The obedient person listens to others to discover what is true and what is good and what should be done. Among those others who should be listened to, some are leaders with authority in the community. They hold the place of Christ in the community. Quite apart from theology, in any community the leaders are likely to be better informed than anyone else, so their decisions have a certain a priori weight. Moreover, the community good is promoted far more often by ready implementation of the leader's orders than by stubborn resistance to them. Benedict says monks should make their ideas known, and if they think they cannot do something they should say so. The abbot should consider their statements, then repeat or reformulate his orders. The monk should obey them. At worst, he will fail; at best he will be stretched beyond his self-defined limits.

Hierarchy and obedience are logically distinct. Neither word has a nice ring to it. Hierarchy makes one think of kings; obedience conjures up the Gestapo. In fact, Benedict says monks should obey each other. Three monks should be able to arrange a room without arguing, because their aim is to listen to each other and do God's will, not enforce their own.

Thus obedience looks to the good both of the community and of the individual. For Saint Benedict, one cannot be obedient unless one is also cheerful, and perhaps a bit bemused by the tremendous authority with which people, oneself included, invest their opinions and desires about almost anything, from liturgical minutiae to how to wash the dishes.

Christ is the model of obedience. He sought his father's will and followed where it led. In his case, it led to the cross. Hildegard's personified obedience speaks with the voice of Old Testament Wisdom, and the New Testament Word.

The Benedictine tradition prefers listening to ascetic feats, simple obedience to arrogant ecstasy. The important thing, again, is not what one does, but how one does it.

Truthfully, my children, I tell you that everyone who delights in his own will and is subdued to his own thoughts, and takes up the things sown in his own heart, and rejoices in them, and supposes in his heart that these are some great chosen mystery, and justifies himself in what he does—the soul of such a man is the breath of evil spirits.

ANTONY, *LETTERS*

When we live in community, let us choose obedience over discipline; for the latter teaches arrogance, while the former calls for humility.

LIFE OF SYNCLETICA

Willingly accept the advice of a loving father and put it into action. In that way you will return by the labor of obedience to him whom you left by the inertia of disobedience.

RULE OF BENEDICT

Hate your own will. Obey the commands of the abbot even if he act otherwise.

RULE OF BENEDICT

The primary path to humility is prompt obedience. This befits those who hold nothing dearer to them than Christ. . . . It is a desire for eternal life that motivates them.

RULE OF BENEDICT

Obedience extended to one's superior is given to God, for he himself said: "Whoever listens to you listens to me" [Lk 10.16]. This must be done by disciples with a willing mind, because "God loves a cheerful giver" [2 Cor 9.7].

RULE OF BENEDICT

The second step of humility is reached when someone who does not love his own will does not delight in fulfilling his own desires, but imitates with his deeds the saying of the Lord: "I have not come to do my own will, but the will of him who sent me" [Jn 6.38].

RULE OF BENEDICT

The third step of humility is that someone, out of love for God, submit himself in all obedience to his superior, imitating the Lord, of whom the Apostle says: "He was made obedient unto death" [Phil 2.8].

RULE OF BENEDICT

We rightly learn not to do our own will when we are frightened by what holy Scripture says: "There are ways that seem right to men, but whose end is plunged in the depths of hell" [Prov 16.25].

RULE OF BENEDICT

The eighth step of humility is that the monk do nothing that is not enjoined by the common rule of the monastery or the examples of the elders.

RULE OF BENEDICT

When someone is newly come to monastic life, easy entrance should not be granted him. . . . One should take note whether he really seeks God, if he is serious about the work of God [liturgical prayer], obedience, and hardships. . . . One to be received [into the community] must promise stability, fidelity to the monastic lifestyle, and obedience in front of all in the chapel.

RULE OF BENEDICT

If burdensome or impossible tasks are enjoined on a brother, let him accept the command of the superior meekly and obediently. But if the burden of the task seems to exceed completely the limits of his strength, let him mention to the one giving the order the causes of his incapacity and do so patiently and at the proper time, without pride, obstinacy, or refusal. But if, after his suggestion, the superior does not change his mind, let him know that it is for his own good, and obey out of love, trusting in God's help.

RULE OF BENEDICT

Not only is the blessing of obedience to be shown to the abbot by all, but they are also to obey each other, knowing that by this road of obedience they will go to God.

RULE OF BENEDICT

[Obedience says:] Just as a human being's will perfects whatever she desires, so am I the will in God, by bringing to fulfillment what God commands. I was with God in his primordial council. God arranged all things through me, whatever he wanted to do. For I responded to the command of his word just like a lyre, because I am his command. I touch nothing, wish nothing, desire nothing, except what is in God, for I came forth from him, and I grew through him; I want nothing besides God.

HILDEGARD OF BINGEN,
BOOK OF LIFE'S MERITS

Whoever wishes to offer God an acceptable sacrifice has nothing more precious to offer than his own will.

JOHN TRITHEMIUS, *RULE*

It is better to sweep up leaves out of simple obedience than to engage in the sublime contemplation of heavenly things out of self-will.

LOUIS DE BLOIS, *SPIRITUAL MIRROR*

Monastic obedience exists not to make yes-men and efficient bureaucrats who can be used in institutional politics, but to liberate the hearts and minds into the lucid and terrible darkness of a contemplation that no tongue can explain and no rationalization can account for.

THOMAS MERTON,
CONTEMPLATION IN A WORLD OF ACTION

The monastic vocation really allows quite a lot of scope for individual differences, at least it should allow quite a lot of scope for the individual to follow a personal call, to follow something that he feels is especially relevant to him.

THOMAS MERTON,
CONTEMPLATION IN A WORLD OF ACTION

Mere outward compliance will not do. Obedience should come cheerfully, freely, and gladly. It is only when I remind myself that obedience is *ob-audiens,* listening intently to God rather than listening to my own self, that what Benedict is telling me—even though it may still seem difficult—is not impossible, for it is a response of love to love.

ESTHER DE WAAL, *A LIFE-GIVING WAY*

Christ's obedience was obedience unto death. This gives me the perspective. I am being asked to let go of something in me that must die before the new can be born. Two things help to make this possible: that the motive force is love; that I do it in imitation of Christ.

ESTHER DE WAAL, *A LIFE-GIVING WAY*

Obedience depends on listening so totally and openly to the other that through them we discern the face, the voice of

Christ himself. This is the root of that obedience that we show to one another.

ESTHER DE WAAL, *A LIFE-GIVING WAY*

No one grows simply by doing what someone else forces us to do. We begin to grow when we finally want to grow.

SR. JOAN CHITTISTER,
THE RULE OF BENEDICT

Obedience, Benedict says—the willingness to listen for the voice of God in life—is what will wrench us out of the limitations of our own landscape.

SR. JOAN CHITTISTER,
THE RULE OF BENEDICT

CHAPTER 16

Authority

A whole theory of effective management could be derived from the monastic tradition. Christian monasticism could also provide countless examples of good and bad managers. Benedict himself seems to have failed when, with no experience of community life, he was made abbot of an existing community. By the time he established Monte Cassino, he had learned management by study and by trial and error. For example, when in the *Rule* he becomes strident about the dangers of having a prior, especially one appointed by the same people who appoint the abbot, he seems to be animated by some unpleasant memories.

The authority of the desert fathers and mothers who served as guides to other hermits was based on their perceived wisdom and virtue. The disciple whose needs were no longer met by one spiritual guide could move on to another. With the advent of community life, relations between *abba* or *amma* and the individual monastics under them were transformed. The *abba* or *amma* was now the leader of a community, and the monastic's commitment was now to a community to which he or she was permanently attached. Moreover, the *abba* or *amma* was now responsible for both the spiritual and temporal welfare of the community. Many an abbot would experience tensions between institutional and personal need—for example, between the need to appoint an administrator for some important monastic enterprise and the felt need of the only possible appointee for solitude or manual work or serving others directly and personally in the infirmary or the guest house or the school.

When they became abbots or bishops or popes, the responsibilities of some monks became enormous. Saint Bernard's protégé Eugene III found the papacy almost overwhelming. Bernard advised him to use his time wisely, to delegate, to surround himself with trustworthy helpers, and above all to take time to examine himself to make sure he was acting thoughtfully and fairly.

The *Life of Pachomius* offers the example of a very skillful leader and manager who could read hearts, organize communities, and plan for the future. Pachomius could deal effectively with people because he was not handicapped by concerns for his own dignity or prerogatives. Although Pachomius's efforts to train a successor were only partially successful, he did make the attempt. He knew, as any abbot or parent knows, that one must share responsibility if one is to nurture leadership for the next generation. One of Pachomius's immediate successors enunciated a principle that is applicable in most ecclesiastical settings: if a person desires power, that person probably should not be given authority.

The entire monastic tradition teaches that whoever is in charge should teach by word and example. She must adapt herself to different temperaments, but not play favorites. She should be especially devoted to the delinquent and the needy. Positions of responsibility should be awarded according to the merit of the candidates' behavior and wise teaching. Benedict insists that his subordinate officials treat the rest of the community fairly. They are not to meddle in what is not their concern. Like the abbot, they should seek to be loved rather than to be feared.

Although the *Rule of Benedict* gives great authority to the abbot, there are evident limits. Benedict's *Rule* places the abbot under the *Rule,* while making the *Rule* and the abbot the normative guides for the monks. The *Rule* legislates that the abbot should not make decisions without consulting members of the community, and that he should not make major decisions without consulting all of the community. Thus does the community help the abbot discern what is God's will. Deliberate deception through manipulative internal or external public relations, privileged access to information or to the seats of power, disdain for procedures, and all the other tricks of political expediency are diametrically opposed to this communal effort at discernment.

The *Rule* says that the abbot *"is believed* to hold the place of Christ." Effective monastic government is rooted in faith not in the abbot primarily, though trust between abbot and monks is crucial, but in the God of the covenant who leads the people according to the divine promises. The God who inspired Syncletica and Benedict and the members of their communities inspires their successors today.

Remembering the promise he had made to God, Pachomius began with his brother to build a larger monastery to receive those who would come to this life. As they were building, Pachomius was extending the place with this aim in view while his brother, thinking of withdrawal apart, was making it smaller. And once John, who was older according to the flesh, was vexed and said to him, "Stop being conceited!" When Pachomius heard this he became angry as if for a good cause, but did not say anything in reply to him. As he kept control of his heart, he went down to a little cavern during the following night and began to weep in sorrow. He prayed, "O God, the mind of the flesh is still in me. . . . But I believe that if your many mercies help me I will be taught henceforth to walk in the way of the saints, 'stretching out towards what lies ahead' [Phil 3.13]. For with your help they put the enemy to shame as they ought. And how will I teach those whom you call to choose this life with me, O Lord, if I have not first conquered myself?"

LIFE OF PACHOMIUS

The father of a nearby monastery used to visit the holy father, Pachomius. One of his monks was asking for the rank of steward, but he did not consider him worthy of that task. Not being able to persuade him, he told him guilefully, "Our father Pachomius warned me not to do this, knowing well that you are not yet worthy of your request." When he heard this, the brother dragged him along angrily, saying, "Come, let us go to him, and he shall have to prove what he says against me!" The other followed him in fear and sorrow, wondering what the result of that affair would be.

When they arrived, they found Pachomius with the brothers, building a wall for the monastery. That brother approached Pachomius and told him very angrily, "Come down, liar, and give me a proof of my sin!" As [Pachomius] kept silent, he said to him again, "Is your mouth silenced, finding nothing in your defense? Who compels you to lie, you who claim to be clairvoyant, when you are stone-blind?" When he had said this, the Great Man answered, knowing nothing of what the other was talking about, "I have sinned against you: forgive me. Have you never trans-gressed?" When he heard this his anger calmed down.

The Old Man came down from his work and sought the father of the other monastery. He found him weeping and heart-broken, and he asked him, "What is going on?" He answered, "This brother has asked us for a ministry beyond his worth. I knew I could not make him give up his claim, for he does not listen to me. So I used your name to quiet him down, for we know that the Lord has granted you the gift of discovering guile swiftly. And behold this fool has added to his evil deeds by reviling a righteous man." Pachomius said to him, "Have you not come to seek from me the will of God? Listen to me. Grant him his request that by this means we may snatch his soul away from the en-emy. For it happens when good is done to a bad man he may come to some perception of the good. This is God's love, to have compassion for each other."

When that brother had got what he wanted, he returned immediately to the great Pachomius, greatly sobered. He embraced him and confessed, "O Man of God, you are much greater than we had heard. We have seen how you have conquered evil with good by sparing a foolish sinner like me. If you had not been truly patient and had said something against me, I would have rejected the monastic life and become estranged from God. Blessed are you, for thanks to you, I live."

LIFE OF PACHOMIUS

Another time the brothers were with [Pachomius] cutting rushes. And as they were transporting the rushes to the boat, Pachomius suddenly fell into ecstasy. He saw some of the brothers surrounded by a fiery circle with flames licking them, and they were unable to pass over it. Others were barefoot on top of thorny pieces of wood, pierced by splinters, and they had no way out. And others were standing half-way up a steep precipice, unable either to climb up or to throw themselves into the river, for there were crocodiles below, watching them and leaping up at them. As he was still standing there, taken by his vision, the brothers passing by saw him. They cast their burdens down and they stood by him in prayer.

When he returned to himself after a long hour, he ordered food to be given to the brothers, for it was already evening. Then he told them to gather around him. He told them about his vision and they all wept with great fear. And as they asked him what this meant, he said, "I perceive that after my death this will happen to the brothers, who will not find anyone capable of comforting them rightly in the Lord from their afflictions."

LIFE OF PACHOMIUS

Abba Pachomius loved Theodore because he bore the life well. . . . He appointed him housemaster of the Alexandrians and foreigners who came after him. And his house was full of piety.

The holy Pachomius did many things with him, instructing him how to govern men. He would say, "It is a great thing! If you see someone of the house negligent of his salvation, admonish him privately with patience. If he once gets angry, leave him until God moves him to repentance. It is just like when someone wants to extract a thorn from somebody's foot. He digs around it, and if it bleeds and is painful, it is better to leave it and to put on it a softening plaster or something similar. Then after a few days it comes out by itself and easily. A man who is angry even against someone who does not argue with him will gain more after this from the one who is teaching him according to the Law. But if the offense is serious, report it to us and we will do as the merciful Lord wants. Care also for the sick as for your- self. Practice continence and bear the cross more than they do, since you hold the rank of father. And be the first to keep the rules of the brothers so that they also may keep them. And if after this there is anything else you want to de- cide and you do not know how, by the grace of God tell me about it. Together we shall try to find the exact answer to each one of the problems."

LIFE OF PACHOMIUS

Here is also what our father Horsiesios used to say, "I see some of you wanting to receive titles and to rule. . . . In the past, in the time of our father [Pachomius], except in obedi- ence, nobody wanted to be called great, fearing to be found least in the kingdom of heaven [Mt 5.19]. And when Abba Petronios appointed me, I wept copiously, in fear of the dan- ger to souls. Not only I, but the saints also. Moses, being sent by God for the sake of the people, first declined in his humil- ity, and then accepted that ministry only when God was an- gered at him because of this. As for us, brothers, hearing what is written, "He who exalts himself will be humbled" [Lk 18.14], let us watch ourselves. It does not belong to all to govern souls, but only to perfect men. Here is a parable: if an unbaked brick is set in a foundation near a river, it does not last a single day; but if it is baked, it endures like stone.

LIFE OF PACHOMIUS

The abbot is believed to hold the place of Christ in the monastery.

RULE OF BENEDICT

When someone receives the title "abbot," he must direct his disciples with a twofold teaching; that is, he should show all that is good and holy more by his deeds than by his words.

RULE OF BENEDICT

There should be no playing favorites in the monastery.

RULE OF BENEDICT

Let the abbot be aware what a difficult and arduous task he has taken up: to govern souls and put himself at the service of many different temperaments, one with encouraging words, another with rebukes, another with persuasion.

RULE OF BENEDICT

Fearing always the judgment that awaits the shepherd regarding the sheep entrusted to him, let the account [the abbot] must give of others make him careful about himself, so that when he admonishes others he will also amend his own bad inclinations.

RULE OF BENEDICT

Whenever some important matters are to be dealt with in the monastery, let the abbot convene the entire community and tell them what is to be considered, and hearing the council of the brothers, let him ponder the matter and do what he judges is most expedient. The reason we said all should be called to council is that the Lord often reveals to the youngest what is best.

RULE OF BENEDICT

In all things let all follow the rule as master, and let no one depart from it rashly. No one in the monastery should simply follow the will of his heart.

RULE OF BENEDICT

If the community be larger, let there be chosen from it brothers of good repute and holy life, and let them be

appointed as deans who will take care of their deaneries
in all things according to the commands of God and the
precepts of their abbot. Those chosen to be deans should be
such that the abbot can confidently share his burdens with
them. They should be chosen . . . for their deserving lives
and wise teaching.

RULE OF BENEDICT

The abbot should exercise great care regarding delinquent
brothers, for it is not the healthy who need a doctor but
those who are sick [cf. Mt 9.12]. . . . He should understand
that he has undertaken to care for the weak and not to dominate the strong. . . . Let him imitate the devoted example
of the good shepherd, who left the ninety-nine sheep in the
mountains, and went to seek the one sheep that had wan-
dered off [cf. Lk 15.4–5].

RULE OF BENEDICT

A cellarer of the monastery should be chosen from the community—a person wise, of mature character, and sober in
judgment. He should not be given to excessive eating, nor
proud, nor unfair, nor stingy, nor wasteful. He should fear
God and be like a father to the whole community. He
should care for the needs of all, but he should not do anything without the abbot's command.

RULE OF BENEDICT

The cellarer should not embarrass the brothers. If a brother
should make an unreasonable request, he should not brush
him off and hurt his feelings, but deny the unjustified request reasonably and humbly.

RULE OF BENEDICT

In the installation of an abbot, the proper procedure is always to appoint whoever is chosen by the whole community in accord with the fear of God. Let the candidate be

selected because of his worthy life and wise doctrine, even if he is the last in seniority.

RULE OF BENEDICT

The abbot should keep in mind what kind of burden he has accepted and to whom he is going to render an account of his stewardship. He should know that it is more important for him to be of profit to his monks than to preside over them. It is necessary therefore that he be learned in the divine law so that he may know how to bring forth things new and old; that he be chaste, temperate, and merciful . . . He should hate vices and love the community. In correcting, he should act prudently and not overdo it.

RULE OF BENEDICT

Let the abbot strive to be loved more than to be feared.

RULE OF BENEDICT

The abbot should not be restless and worried, nor extreme and stubborn, nor jealous and overly suspicious, because then he will never have peace.

RULE OF BENEDICT

He should be farseeing and thoughtful, discerning and moderate.

RULE OF BENEDICT

[Young Wulfstan] was serious of mind and speech, reverent, cheerful; he wore the clothes of a layman, but lived like a monk. If he saw someone in need of correction, he always tempered his speech, so that the rigor of harsh correction might be followed by some reason for praise. He could hardly appear harsh, because although what he said might be strict, it was inwardly scented with love.

LIFE OF WULFSTAN

[When Wulfstan was made prior] he showed striking zeal in solidifying the external possessions of the monastery, which his predecessors had let deteriorate, and he reformed the internal life within the boundaries of the *Rule*. In order to do this effectively, he offered to those under him the devout example of his own life. He was ashamed to preach anything that he hesitated to put into practice.

LIFE OF WULFSTAN

The holy man Wulfstan was presented at the court of the king. He was ordered to accept the gift of the office of bishop. He resisted, saying he was unworthy to receive such an honor. Meanwhile, all the rest called out that he was worthy. . . . The cardinals and archbishops would have labored in vain to convince him to accept the office if they had not countered his resistance with the duty to obey the pope. . . . The more he thought himself unworthy, the more insistent was the people's urging. For he showed more promise of being a wise administrator because he came to the task not without fear. A fool takes on a task heedlessly, ignorant of how much work it will require.

LIFE OF WULFSTAN

If someone came to him for advice, he thoughtfully gave it. If someone made a request, he was very approachable. When some request had to be answered, he deliberated fairly and announced his decision quickly. When he had to pass judgment, he sided with justice. He did not tap the rich for money, nor repulse the poor because of their poverty. He was unmoved by flattery, and not obliged to those who flattered him. He never swerved from justice because of fear of princes, nor did he, for love of them, give them any honor they did not deserve. When he was praised for his goodness, he attributed it to the grace of God and was not proud. When he was criticized, he forgave the error of those who criticized him, at ease with his conscience. Criticism came his way rarely, because he cherished every man with a father's love; in turn, all loved him as if he were a parent.

LIFE OF WULFSTAN

There are many who live peacefully under a superior until the yoke is lifted. Then they cannot be quiet, nor keep themselves from disturbing their equals. Similarly, you see countless people who can live with their brothers without any conflict, but when they are placed over their brothers they are not only useless but foolish and wicked. People like this must be satisfied with a moderate level of goodness, in accord with the measure of grace that God has granted them. They do not need a master, but they are not suited to be masters, either. The latter excel the former somewhat in character, but there are those who excel them both because they know how to be superiors. Finally they are entrusted with all the Lord's goods. But there are few who can preside effectively, fewer yet who can preside humbly. The person who is perfectly schooled in discretion, the mother of the virtues, can fulfill both roles easily.

BERNARD OF CLAIRVAUX,
ON THE SONG OF SONGS

When you ponder your present state, you should also recall how you used to be. Compare your present state with your past one. Have you grown in virtue, in wisdom, in under-standing? Are you easier to get along with? . . . Reflect upon your zeal, your mercy, and also your discretion. . . . Reflect on the way you forgive and punish injuries, and in each consider how carefully you take into account manner, place, and time. . . . In addition, I do not want you to over-look the way you act in tribulations.

BERNARD OF CLAIRVAUX,
ON CONSIDERATION

Preside in order to promote the good of those whom you govern. . . . Provide rather than dominate. I fear for you, for there is no poison more dangerous . . . , nor sword more deadly, than the lust to dominate.

BERNARD OF CLAIRVAUX,
ON CONSIDERATION

Accept no secret and murmured accusations. Think of them rather as detractions. I would like you to make this a general rule for yourself, that you hold suspect everyone who fears to say openly what he has whispered in your ear.

BERNARD OF CLAIRVAUX,
ON CONSIDERATION

Good teachers . . . govern their students with discernment and with fair correction.

HILDEGARD OF BINGEN,
BOOK OF LIFE'S MERITS

Fathers, do not grow tired of caring for your sheep. Nothing is more acceptable to God than the service of pastoral care. God requires of pastors that, as a sign of Christ's love, they feed the sheep entrusted to them with diligent care. . . . Accept with fearless humility the talent given you. You can be *fearless* because you have as a helper the very one who sent you. You will be consoled by the one who urged the fearful Moses to assume care of a great and burdensome people: "Go, I will be with you." And Christ prayed for Peter: "I have asked on your behalf, Peter, that your faith not fail and that when you have devoted yourself to the care committed to you, you may strengthen them as I have already strengthened you." . . . You should be *humble,* for no one should presume he can feed the flocks on his own, for God foresaw that he would need great, divine prayers.

LUDOVICO BARBO, *LETTERS*

Never forget our holy Father [Benedict's dictum]: strive to be loved by your sons rather than feared. If you wish to be loved, love! A superior who loves fosters virtues with good and frequent exhortations and nurtures spiritual progress. He corrects the erring, not as an angry judge, but as a loving father.

LUDOVICO BARBO, *LETTERS*

Where there is mildness in the father (superior), there will be no distrust; if mildness is combined with care, there no sin can take root. Where these are combined with prudence, there is no meaningless correction. For the correction given by a kind, solicitous, and prudent father is received with love, works in due time, and brings a suitable healing to wounds.

LUDOVICO BARBO, *LETTERS*

Since "the art of arts is the government of souls," as Gregory says in his *Pastoral Rule,* wretched is the one who is compelled to teach before he has a chance to learn, who is forced to show to others a way he has never walked.

JOHN TRITHEMIUS, *RULE*

Who would not rather feed some farmer's pigs than have governance over souls?

JOHN TRITHEMIUS, *RULE*

Just as the superior must be very diligent in correcting faults, so he must be particularly discreet. Let him always note what sort of fault it is, whether it was done knowingly or ignorantly, whether it was committed only once or often, whether it was humbly admitted or proudly defended.

LOUIS DE BLOIS, *STATUTES*

Now there must be a very delicate balancing between the superior and his personal gifts, the insights of the living community and the Rule that is the bearer of the accumulated wisdom of tradition. . . . Openness to the working of the Spirit in both individual and in community is vital, lifegiving. Without it, there will be a closed-up person, a closed-up community, lacking the growth that Benedict holds out so urgently in the prologue.

ESTHER DE WAAL,
A LIFE-GIVING WAY

The cellarer is said to be like *(sicut)* a father to the community. But that word *sicut* is important. He is not to take over the role of the head of the community; he is a man under orders. Benedict knows only too well that for anyone who has to deal with material possessions, there is always the danger of the abuse of power.

ESTHER DE WAAL,
A LIFE-GIVING WAY

The superior of a monastery of Benedictines will be a Christ figure, simple, unassuming, immersed in God, loving of the marginal, doer of the Gospel, beacon to the strong.

SR. JOAN CHITTISTER,
THE RULE OF BENEDICT

[Benedict] does not want people in positions simply to get a job done. He wants people in positions who embody why we bother to do the job at all. He wants holy listeners who care about the effect of what they do on everybody else.

SR. JOAN CHITTISTER,
THE RULE OF BENEDICT

It is not easy for honest people who hold their own failures in their praying hands to question behavior in anyone else. . . . Aware of what I myself am capable of doing, how can I possibly censure or disparage or reprimand or reproach anyone else? On the other hand, Benedict reminds us, how can those who know that conversion is possible, who have been called to midwife the spiritual life, for this generation and the next, do less?

SR. JOAN CHITTISTER,
THE RULE OF BENEDICT

Abbots and prioresses, good leaders and teachers, fine parents and mentors, tender husbands and gentle wives, good friends and quality administrators, who listen to us as much as we listen to them, are there to help us bear the heat of life that shapes us, not to escape it.

SR. JOAN CHITTISTER,
THE RULE OF BENEDICT

[People in positions of authority should] "keep watch over their own souls" guarding themselves against the pitfalls of any position: arrogance, disinterest, unkindness, aloofness from the very people the position is designed to serve. Then, to make the point clear, Benedict describes the people who are not to get overlooked for the sake of efficiency in the bureaucratic game of hurry up and wait. And they are everybody who cannot possibly be expected to want things when the office is open: the sick, the young, the guests, and the poor.

SR. JOAN CHITTISTER,
THE RULE OF BENEDICT

PART THREE

The Good Desired and Possessed

ONE OF THE MOST STRIKING things in monastic writings is the emphasis on desire and longing. A well-ordered, virtuous life was not enough for the monastic writers we have studied here. They desired something greater, someone greater. Their Christian faith guided their desire, but the desire itself seems to be implanted in every person. Order and virtue can become smug, closed, not a place of delight like the garden enclosed of the *Song of Songs,* but a prison. Saint Anselm is the most eloquent spokesman for this abiding discontent, but almost any monastic author would provide suitable texts. Such writers sometimes had recourse to the same *Song of Songs* to express the longing they felt: "I am faint with love." They believed that their desire, no matter how purified, would never be fully at rest in this life, and so they looked from earthly experience to ecstasy and heaven. Not every reader of this book will be able to join monastics on this part of their quest, but most readers will recognize the desire and perhaps join in their hope that love really is stronger than death.

We desire true and everlasting life.

RULE OF BENEDICT

There are all the great wonders that the faithful ponder with devotion constantly, because they proceed from God. The one who made these is God alone, because all good things arise from him and return to him. When God created human beings, God caused them to travel around him like a circle in the spirit of life, so that they also return to him often.

HILDEGARD OF BINGEN,
BOOK OF LIFE'S MERITS

God is like a blacksmith who kindles the fire with a bellows, turns the iron round and round to finish his work. When the human spirit is guided properly along the path of good deeds, it will return to eternal joy, see the purest light, and hear the songs of the angels.

HILDEGARD OF BINGEN,
BOOK OF LIFE'S MERITS

The true creative spirit must be fired with love and with an authentic desire of God. This means, in so many words, that the monastic vocation is one which implicitly, if not explicitly, seeks the experience of union with God.

THOMAS MERTON,
CONTEMPLATION IN A WORLD OF ACTION

[Benedict] does not want a collection of passive ciphers, but a dynamic and alive people. This primary spiritual energy which brings light and fire, passion and fervor and which prevents what might otherwise be simply plodding, he calls "a very ardent love." The Latin *ferventissimo amore* suggests a burning, white-hot love.

ESTHER DE WAAL, *A LIFE-GIVING WAY*

CHAPTER 17

Longing

In a poem about feeling and love, Hadewijch, a devout Beguine of the thirteenth century, echoes much of what the monastic tradition says about longing and desire. To desire many things, to prefer pleasurable feeling, is to aim too low. One must, she says, desire beyond reason. Love causes constant striving until at last desire drowns in sublime love. Desire is too lofty to be at rest in insignificant things. Love itself is its object, and in this life, love is always just out of reach.

The danger, then, is that we amplify our superficial and incidental desires so much that we can't hear our deeper longings. Then we become like addicts going from one fix to the next, unwilling to face the fatal artificiality of our cravings. Renouncing our cravings will not make us apathetic; rather, it will give us wings to fly above the stars. One taste of God, and we will thirst for nothing else.

The one thing necessary is the good we can serve. Even if that good is identical to God himself, we must not promote it with evil means. Evil means bring us to evil ends, not to God. Evil means are infallible signs of disordered desires or of a lack of trust in the power of God to bring about the good he desires.

A man who finds himself in the cold and deep frost runs somehow until he reaches the heat of the fire; then he is delighted and revives. So also was it with us then; the more we sought God, the more his goodness manifested itself, bringing sweetness to our souls. But how are we now? Let us, however, all return; we do believe that God will renew us in his mercy.

LIFE OF PACHOMIUS

Entrust your hope to God.

RULE OF BENEDICT

Never despair of the mercy of God.

RULE OF BENEDICT

With a ready heart and a happy face, he was tasting beforehand the joys of heaven. He was anticipating in hope the fountain of heavenly happiness from which he now drinks everlastingly.

LIFE OF WULFSTAN

Hope and rejoice, rejoice and love, my soul. The one whom you hesitatingly desired to listen to you prepares an intercessor for you. As a beggar, you made your request through another, because you did not have confidence enough to go to him directly. Behold, he came to you and prayed for you where you failed. What goodness, kindness, love. Behold, he showed you how much he loved you, and how much he enkindled in you a love of him. Insist, then, and hope, not in yourself but in him. He will hear your desire who concludes your prayer: " 'Exult in him, my heart and my flesh' [Ps 84.2], love him, and let 'everything within me' [Ps 103.1] bless him. Amen."

ANSELM OF CANTERBURY, PRAYERS

O most kind lover of the human race, . . . manifest your presence and I will have what I desire. Reveal your glory, and my joy will be perfect. "My soul thirsts for you, and my flesh is yours in many ways" [Ps 63.2]. "My soul thirsts for God, the living fountain. When will I come and appear before the face of my God?" [Ps 42.2] When will you come, my consoler, whom I seek? Oh for the time when I will see my joy that I desire! Oh that "I will be satisfied when your glory has appeared" [Ps 17.15], the glory that I crave. Oh that I might be made drunk "with the richness of your house" for which I sigh! If you will only give me to drink from the "torrent of your delight" [Ps 36.8] for which I thirst!

ANSELM OF CANTERBURY, *PRAYERS*

[Hope] understands that hard discipline has an end and that everlasting glory will follow it. After a foretaste of the earnest money, patience will grow sweet; without hope, patience would have been bitter. Boredom will turn into desire, irritation into delight, delay into longing forbearance. [His seven years of labor] seemed like just a few days to Jacob because of his love for Rachel [cf. Gen 29.20].

PETER OF CELLE,
THE SCHOOL OF THE CLOISTER

[Hope says:] I sit on the throne of God desiring good, and in faith I embrace all his works. By doing good works, I draw all the earth to myself.

HILDEGARD OF BINGEN,
BOOK OF LIFE'S MERITS

God . . . will receive me then into the highest bliss; and set me on his lap.

HILDEGARD OF BINGEN,
BOOK OF LIFE'S MERITS

[Heavenly desire declared:] I am the life and greenness in all good works, and a necklace of all the virtues. I am the delight and understanding of the love of God and the upbuilding of his every desire, because whatever God wishes, I do, and with the wings of goodwill I fly above the stars of heaven, so that I bring to perfection the will of God in every just event. . . . I want nothing except what is holy.

HILDEGARD OF BINGEN,
BOOK OF LIFE'S MERITS

Finally, the blessed father [Benedict] affirms all these things; the kingdom of heaven will lie open to those who do them [cf. *Rule of Benedict* 72]. All the things that are described in this rule are neither too slack nor too restrictive; they look neither to the right nor to the left, so that they lead the one who keeps them straight to heaven.

HILDEGARD OF BINGEN,
EXPLANATION OF THE RULE OF BENEDICT

Let me taste the sweetness of your Spirit; make me thirst that your will be done; make me know your good pleasure so that my service may always be acceptable to you. Amen. . . . Ah, Jesus, fountain of life, make me drink a cup of the living water from you so that, having tasted you, I will thirst eternally for nothing but you.

GERTRUDE THE GREAT,
SPIRITUAL EXERCISES

Ah! O beloved of my vows, understand my cry. Direct your attention to my prayer and heed me; for the longing of my heart and the desire of my soul, O my king and my God, call you, want you, and need you. Because of you my eyes are dewed with tears, and my gaze is intent on you. You, my God, my gentleness and love, my hope from my youth: you are all that I want, hope, and desire.

GERTRUDE THE GREAT,
SPIRITUAL EXERCISES

God seeks us with grace and mercy; we seek him with devout feelings, entreating him to heal our misery.

JOHN TRITHEMIUS, *RULE*

The rational spirit is so noble that no perishable good can satisfy it. For the things that are inferior to it cannot satisfy it and make it happy. Inferior to the human spirit are heaven, earth, the sea, and all that is visible or within the range of the senses. Only God, its creator, who is incomparably better and more worthy than it, can make the human spirit content and happy. He wanders like a homeless person with no place to rest, like a starving person without food, as long as he does not embrace with the arms of love him whose greatness he cannot resist desiring.

LOUIS DE BLOIS, *SPIRITUAL DOCTRINE*

First of all, I warn you to think often and carefully about why you entered the monastery—namely, that, dead to the world and to yourself, you might live for God alone.

LOUIS DE BLOIS, *MIRROR FOR MONKS*

God is going to give us an eternal reward for our holy desires, even if in this life we never attained what we desired. So act boldly, keep asking, knock, wait patiently; remember the trustworthy promises of the Lord Jesus, who says: "Everyone who asks, receives, and whoever seeks, finds; to the one knocking the entrance will be opened at a suitable time" [Lk 11.10].

LOUIS DE BLOIS, *SPIRITUAL DOCTRINE*

The worst temptation, and that to which many monks succumb early in their lives, and by which they remained defeated, is simply to give up asking and seeking. To leave everything to the superiors in this life and to God in the next—a hope which may in fact be nothing but a veiled despair, a refusal to live.

THOMAS MERTON,
CONJECTURES OF A GUILTY BYSTANDER

Benedict made it clear that the desire for good is no excuse for the exercise of evil in its behalf. . . . To become what we hate—as mean as the killers, as obsessed as the haters—is neither the goal nor the greatness of the spiritual life.

SR. JOAN CHITTISTER,
THE RULE OF BENEDICT

CHAPTER 18

Love

Near the end of his *Rule*, Benedict recapitulates his teaching:

> Monks should act zealously with a most fervent love—that is, take the
> initiative in showing each other honor, bear patiently weaknesses of
> body and character, vie in obeying one another. Let no one follow
> what he thinks useful for himself, but rather what is to the others' ad-
> vantage. Let them love the brothers chastely; let them fear God out of
> love; let them love their abbot with a sincere and humble love. Let
> them prefer nothing to Christ.

In this brief paragraph Benedict mentions love five times. The
objects of this love are God, Christ, the abbot, and the other members of the community. The qualities of this love are zeal, fervor, dis-
interestedness, sincerity, and humility. It leads to reverence, patience,
and obedience.

The love that Benedict has in mind consists of selfless, active care
and concern for the good of the rest of creation and a grateful surrender of oneself into the hands and purposes of God. Following the
Gospels, the monastic tradition affirms that the commands to love
God above all things and to love one's neighbor as oneself (Mk
12.30–31) are really a single command.

The ordering of time, the virtues that form human character—
these are so many tin soldiers waiting to be brought to life so they can
dance to the music of love. Love is why monasteries are not maintained
to produce paragons of Stoic virtue or still life portraits of imagined
Christs. People who love as the Gospels require aim to be alive, passionate, joyful, and totally given to doing God's will. God wants

people fully alive, wise lovers. Such people want others to become what God wants for them, not carbon copies of themselves. The number of monastic virtues may be finite, but the variety of monastic saints has been quasi-infinite. The discipline of the Lord's school aims to produce discerning and passionate individuals who can represent life for others and be responsible for themselves.

[After struggling with the devil's temptations, Antony] was too feeble to stand, so he prayed lying down. His prayer finished, he called out with a shout: "Here am I, Antony. I am not cowed by your blows. Even though you should give me more, nothing shall separate me from the love of Christ." Then he began to sing: "If armies shall stand against me, my heart shall not fear" [Ps 26.3].

LIFE OF ANTONY

I want you to know this, that Jesus Christ our Lord is himself the true Mind of the Father. By him all the fullness of every rational nature is made in the image of His image. Therefore, we should love one another very much. For he who loves his neighbor, loves God, while whoever loves God, loves his own soul.

LIFE OF ANTONY

[The devils] attack first those who have attained a very great measure. They seek by means of pride and vainglory to turn them against one another. They know that in this way they can cut us off from God, for they know that those who love their neighbors, love God. For this reason, the enemies of virtue sow division in our hearts, that we may be filled with great enmity against each other and not hold any converse with our neighbor, even from a distance.

ANTONY, *LETTERS*

Abba Antony said, "I no longer fear God, but I love him. For love chases out fear" [Jn 4.18].

ANTONY, *SAYINGS*

My children, all of us—male and female—know about being saved, but through our own negligences we stray from the path of salvation. First of all we must observe the precepts known through the grace of the Lord, and these are: "You shall love the Lord your God with your whole soul, and your neighbor as yourself" [Mt 22.37]. In these precepts the first principle of the Law is preserved, and it is on this Law that the fullness of grace depends. The expression of the principle is brief indeed, but its importance in this matter is great and unlimited, for all advice to help the soul depends on these precepts. Paul also bears witness to this when he says that "the end of law is love" [cf. Rom 13.10; 1 Tm 1.5]. Whatever people say by the grace of the Spirit, therefore, that is useful, springs from love and ends in it. Salvation, then, is exactly this—the two-fold love of God and of our neighbor.

LIFE OF *SYNCLETICA*

Love, then, is a great treasure; and about this virtue the Apostle spoke strongly: "If you distribute all your goods, and if you discipline your body, but have not love, you are sounding brass and clanging symbol" [1 Cor 13.1–3]. And so, among the virtues love is paramount.

LIFE OF *SYNCLETICA*

Just as dreadful qualities are attached to one another (for example, envy follows upon avarice, as do treachery, perjury, anger, and remembrance of wrongs), so the opposite qualities of these vices are dependent upon love. I mean, of course, gentleness and patience, as well as endurance, and the ultimate good—holy poverty. It is not possible for anyone to acquire this virtue (I mean, to be sure, love) apart from holy poverty, for the Lord did not enjoin love on one person, but on all. Those, therefore, who have resources must not overlook those who have needs. The workings of love, in fact, are concealed, for it is impossible for a human being to supply the needs of all, but this is the task of God.

LIFE OF SYNCLETICA

From this day forward look to the greater virtue—love, for you have taken up the cross.

LIFE OF SYNCLETICA

Above all, love the Lord God with all your heart, all your soul, all your strength; then, your neighbor as yourself.

RULE OF BENEDICT

Prefer nothing to the love of Christ.

RULE OF BENEDICT

His sister, Scholastica, had been dedicated to the almighty Lord from her infancy. She made it a point to visit her brother once a year. The man of God came down to her at a place not far from the monastery and owned by it. One day she came as usual. Her venerable brother came as well with some disciples. They spent the entire day in praising God and in holy conversation. As night fell they had something to eat. While they were still at table engaged in holy conversation the hour grew late. The holy woman asked him: "I beg you not to leave me tonight, so that we can talk of the joys of heavenly life until dawn." Benedict answered her: "What are you saying, sister? I cannot remain outside my monk's cell."

The weather was so mild that no cloud appeared in the sky.

When the holy nun had heard her brother's refusal, she placed her hands on the table with her fingers intertwined and put her head in her hands and prayed to the Lord. When she raised her head from the table, there was such thunder and lightning and rain that neither Benedict nor the brothers with him could go a step beyond the shelter where they were. For the nun, putting her head in her hands, had poured forth tears, which turned the quiet sky into a flood. The downpour did not follow her tears by much. It was as though prayer, downpour, and the lifting of her head coincided with the thunder, so that at the same moment she lifted her head the downpour occurred. The man of God, seeing that he could not return to the monastery amid lightning, thunder, and downpours, began to be upset and said: "May almighty God save you, sister. What have you done?" She answered him: "I asked you and you did not listen to me. I asked my Lord, and he heard me. Go now if you can, and return to your monastery, leaving me behind." However, he could not leave the roofed-in place, so he who was unwilling to stay stayed unwillingly. They spent the night talking and delighting each other in holy conversations about the spiritual life. . . . It was completely just that she could accomplish more who loved more.

LIFE OF BENEDICT

The love of God made Wulfstan unaware of how hard he was working.

LIFE OF WULFSTAN

The servant is afraid to look his lord in the eye. The hireling hopes to receive from the hand of the lord. The disciple eagerly listens to the master. The son honors his father. But she who seeks a kiss, loves. Among the gifts of nature, this affection of love has the highest place, especially when it returns to its source, which is God.

BERNARD OF CLAIRVAUX,
ON THE SONG OF SONGS

[Wisdom said:] I arranged all things in order, when I made the circuit of the heaven. In the *[Song of] Songs,* I spoke of the love of the creator for the creature and of the creature

for the creator, how the creator adorned the creature when
he made her because he loved her very much, and how the
creature sought a kiss from the creator when she obeyed him
and was obedient to him in all things. The creature received
a kiss from the creator when God gave her everything she
needed. I joined the love of the creator for the creature and
of the creature for the creator to the love and faith by which
God joins man and woman.

HILDEGARD OF BINGEN,
BOOK OF LIFE'S MERITS

Ah, that my soul may choose to know nothing apart from
you, and that, tutored by your grace and instructed by your
anointing, I may progress well, passionately, and powerfully
in the school of your love.

GERTRUDE THE GREAT,
SPIRITUAL EXERCISES

This is our God, who cherishes us with unconquerable
love, with unfathomable charity, with inseparable affection,
who, because of this, took on himself the bodily substance
of our earth to become a spouse and have it as his spouse.
He cherished us with his entire being. To love him is to
have wed him.

GERTRUDE THE GREAT,
SPIRITUAL EXERCISES

Let the depth of your charity absorb me. Let me be sub-
merged into the abyss of the ocean of your most indulgent
devotion. Let me perish in the deluge of your living love
just as a drop perishes in the depth of the ocean's fullness.
Let me die, let me die in the torrent of your immense
mercy, just as the spark of fire dies in the stream's strongest
current. Let the raindrops of your love envelop me. Let the
cup of your love carry away my life. Let the secret counsel of
your most wise love effect and perfect my glorious death in

life-sustaining love. There, there, I will lose my life in you where you live eternally, O my love, God of my life. Amen.

GERTRUDE THE GREAT,
SPIRITUAL EXERCISES

As iron plunged into fire becomes totally fire, so [Gertrude] enkindled by divine love became wholly love, which desired the salvation of all.

GERTRUDE THE GREAT,
THE HERALD OF DIVINE LOVE

On Christmas, Christ told Gertrude: "Just as I am the image of the substance of God the Father [Heb 1.3] in regard to divinity, so you will be the image of my substance in regard to human nature, for you shall receive in your deified soul the rays of my divinity, just as the air receives the sun's rays. Penetrated to the depths of your heart by this unifying light, you will become capable of more intimate union with me."

GERTRUDE THE GREAT,
THE HERALD OF DIVINE LOVE

Love is the first virtue. Love is required of each believer; whatever is not done in love merits nothing. Next comes joy, so that we may serve the Lord, not in bitterness, but happily.

JOHN TRITHEMIUS, *RULE*

Happy is that soul which strives constantly to purify its heart and to turn within itself, and entirely renounces all self-love, self-will, and self-seeking. Such a one deserves to come closer and closer to God. Finally, when its highest powers have been elevated, illumined, and adorned with divine grace, it will attain unity and simplicity of spirit and will reach love without pictures and a simple knowledge without thinking. Now, when it is capable of receiving a wondrous and ineffable grace of God, it is led to that living font which

flows eternally and is more than adequate to completely refresh the minds of the saints. . . . When, with the power of
love, the intellect rises above all images and is led above itself
(something that only God can grant), it flows from itself
into God. Then God is its peace and enjoyment. . . . Completely enkindled with the fire of divine love, and completely liquefied, it passes into God and, united to him
without a medium, is made one spirit with him, just as gold
and brass are fused into one lump of metal.

LOUIS DE BLOIS, *SPIRITUAL DOCTRINE*

In the course of monastic living and believing, your heart is
enlarged with the inexpressible delight of love and you run
along the way of God's commandments [*Rule of Benedict*
prologue 49]—surely one of the most incomparable phrases
of all time.

ESTHER DE WAAL, *A LIFE-GIVING WAY*

Biographical Sketches

ANSELM OF CANTERBURY (CA. 1033–1109)

Saint Anselm was born in Aosta in northern Italy. A poor relationship with his father troubled his youth. Eventually he went to France, where his mother had relatives. He studied at the monastery of Bec in Normandy, where Lanfranc, another Italian, was the chief teacher. Anselm entered that monastery in 1059. In 1063 he succeeded Lanfranc as head of the school and prior. His was the most brilliant intellect since Augustine, and he was soon a renowned teacher. He was dedicated to the monastic ideal, so much so that he could scarcely imagine any other path to salvation. His writings cover many genres: closely reasoned theological monographs on specific philosophical and theological topics, letters, and prayers. He was elected abbot of Bec in 1078. Fifteen years later Anselm reluctantly agreed to succeed Lanfranc as archbishop of Canterbury. Anselm was not a supple diplomat, and his relations with the Anglo-Norman kings of England were often strained. As a result he spent much of the next fifteen years in exile. In part because exile provided him with leisure, he was able to continue his theological writing. In 1098 he completed *Cur Deus Homo? (Why Did God Become Man?)*, which has rivaled his *Proslogium* (1078–1079) in popularity and influence.

Anselm is represented here by excerpts from his *Prayers and Meditations,* among the most beautiful writings in Christian Latin. In particular, his prayers are suffused with the spirit of the psalms, especially those psalms that express a longing of the human heart for the vision and peace of God. The emotion Anselm expresses in his prayers makes him a significant figure in the transition from the stately and rather detached prayer forms of the first millennium to the more emotional forms of prayer that came after him and were cultivated in Cistercian and Franciscan circles.

ANTONY (CA. A.D. 251–356)

Antony died in A.D. 356. If he lived to the age of 105, as several ancient authors claim, he was born in 251. We know him through three basic sources: a collection of sayings, seven letters, and an influential biography written by the patriarch of Alexandria, Athanasius, who was a very important figure in the struggle against the heresy of Arianism. Athanasius wrote his *Life of Antony* in Greek, but it was soon translated into Latin and became widely known throughout the Christian world. Because of the popularity of this work, Antony is traditionally regarded as the first monk, whereas it is clear from the *Life* itself that there were monks and nuns before him.

Antony was a pious boy who lost his parents when he was still a youth. When he was twenty, he was moved by the New Testament's call to leave all and follow Christ. He divested himself of his property and sent his younger sister to live with some nuns. He put himself under the tutelage of an experienced monk. To find solitude, in 285 he entered a deserted fortress, where he stayed for twenty years. After going to Alexandria during a persecution in 311–313, he retreated deeper into the Egyptian desert. His surviving letters to various monasteries date from 340 or slightly before.

Antony and Athanasius lived during a time of crisis in Egyptian civilization. The distinction between city and countryside was blurring. There was migration to the cities and efforts to flee taxes and other civic obligations. The early monks seem to have come from among elites who had lost their positions or from the new middle classes. Greeks and Copts were intermingling and intermarrying. Traditional Egyptian religion, now mixed with many foreign elements, was challenged by Christianity and gnosticism. It is possible that monks from Christian and gnostic traditions lived peacefully in close proximity, concerned more about ascetic practice than doctrinal clarity. However, Athanasius's Antony will have no truck with heretics.

Athanasius's *Life of Antony* presents the author's ideal monk, an ascetic—that is, someone who led an austere life of self-denial. Antony supported the lawful bishops, avoided or actively opposed heretics, and willingly left doctrinal arguments to the bishops and theologians. Athanasius says Antony's memory, full of Scripture passages, served him in place of books. Nevertheless, the seven letters attributed to Antony suggest that he was an educated man who was strongly influenced by the theology stemming from the brilliant third-century theologian Origen, some of whose speculative ideas were rejected by later theological orthodoxy.

The sayings of Antony included in the collections of sayings by the desert monks and nuns corroborate Athanasius's picture of a wise ascetic who learned his wisdom experientially in struggling against the obstacles presented by the world, the flesh, and the devil. On the basis of this experience, he became a person of great discernment, someone who could detect the work of the devil in the human soul and devise ways of resisting it. His discretion also took the form of moderating his asceticism. Although Athanasius's descriptions of his privations are scarcely conceivable to a modern reader, Athanasius insists that Antony was a specimen of good health, as indeed he must have been if he lived to be 105.

Antony, like many monks celebrated in later saints' lives, was said to have the virtues of the just of the Old Testament—for example, the purity of heart of Elijah. When he emerged from his twenty years in the abandoned fort, he was totally self-controlled—an ideal that some of the monks adopted from Hellenistic philosophy. At times, this domination of the "passions" bordered on disdain of the body.

Athanasius says that Antony was ashamed to give attention to the body or to be seen undressed or eating. Yet he makes clear the Christological basis of Antony's monasticism: all should prefer nothing to the love of Christ.

According to Athanasius, one day Antony addressed the monks at length. He recommended following the Scriptures, consulting a spiritual guide, and perseverance. He urged them not to hesitate to give up temporal goods, however great, for the prospect of eternal goods. To this end he urged them to practice four cardinal virtues (prudence, justice, temperance, and fortitude), as well as understanding, charity, love of the poor, faith in Christ, meekness, and hospitality. Monks should live as men about to die. They should pray to receive through the Holy Spirit the ability to discern spirits. At the end of Antony's discourse, he and the rest of the monks returned to their cells. Theirs was a land apart, inhabited by ascetics seeking virtue, singing psalms, studying, fasting, praying, working, loving each other, and rejoicing in the life to come—and there were no tax collectors.

Later, when Antony moved to his inner mountain, he made friends with the wild animals who were destroying his garden. In later hagiography, monks will always be friends with animals—lambs who lie down peacefully with wolves in the paradise that they create in the desert.

Athanasius's portrait of Antony became a kind of narrative rule for monks. His story of Antony loomed large over subsequent monastic hagiography and provided guidelines for monastic rules. That Antony's virtues and struggles, his admonitions and observances, continue to serve as paradigms is a tribute to Athanasius's vivid recital of Antony's life and teaching.

LUDOVICO BARBO (1381–1443)

The later Middle Ages were not a golden era for monasticism. Few new monasteries were founded, and many of those that existed had difficulties with recruiting, observance, and finances. At the dawning of the modern world the monasteries were not well positioned to come to terms with the new order of emerging nation-states and increasing secular autonomy in economics and learning. However, during the fifteenth century a number of reform-minded Christians struggled to bring new life to monasteries as part of a renewal of the church in leadership and members. Louis (Ludovico) Barbo was one of these reform-minded Christians whose efforts led to the Protestant and Catholic Reformations.

Barbo was born in Venice. At the age of sixteen he was a cleric and commendatory prior (lay overseer) of the Augustinian monastery of Saint Giorgio in Alga, near Venice. His income from this monastery helped pay for his studies in law school. He had a religious conversion in 1403, which moved him to give the monastery of Saint Giorgio to a group of devout clerics. That group included two cousins who were nephews of the pope, both of whom became cardinals and one of whom became Pope Eugene IV. Also associated with the group was Lawrence Giustiniani, who became patriarch of Venice.

In 1408, with papal approval, Barbo was entrusted with the Benedictine abbey of Saint Justina in Padua. The newly appointed abbot first secured from the pope a guarantee that the abbey would be free of all lay interference or control (thus putting an end to the commendatory lay overseers, for whom monasteries were often nothing more than a source of income for themselves). He made his profession as a Benedictine before a bishop and was blessed as abbot in 1409. His first steps were difficult; few men entered the community. Little by little recruitment improved as men were drawn by the serene and stable life of the revived community and Barbo's kindness and discretion. Other monasteries adopted his reforming ideas and practices, and gradually there emerged a congregation of monasteries. In 1419, Pope Martin V approved the new congregation. It was distinguished by the fact that the authority of the congregation was emphasized more than the autonomy of the individual monasteries. Supreme authority lay with the four visitators, who executed the decrees of the annual general chapter. In 1425 Pope Eugene IV approved the practice of electing abbots at the general chapter. Both of these measures were radical departures from the earlier Benedictine tradition of autonomous monastic communities led by abbots of their own choosing. Moreover, the time in office of abbots and other officials was limited by statute.

In making these innovations, Barbo was trying to give greater stability to his precarious work of reform. He was probably also inspired by some then-current ideas about the superiority of a general council over the pope. On papal orders, Barbo wrote a letter about his reforms to the Spanish Benedictine Congregation of Valladolid.

Barbo was named bishop of Treviso in 1437. There he founded a school for poor clerics that anticipated the Tridentine institution of seminaries. He died at the monastery of Saint Giorgio Maggiore in Venice in 1443, and was buried at Saint Justina.

In 1440, Barbo wrote a history of the beginnings of the Congregation of Saint Justina. About the same time he wrote *The Form of Prayer and Meditation of the Congregation of the Monks of Saint Justina* to help implement a decree of the congregation requiring its members to practice mental prayer each day. The work distinguishes three steps of prayer. The first consists of vocal prayers directed to twelve specific saints, asking their help in acquiring particular virtues. The second step consists of affective mental prayer—that is, spontaneous acts of devotion. Barbo specifies for each day some stage or event in the life of Christ that is to stimulate proper devotion. These are assigned for each day of the week; for example, Christ's sufferings are the topic for Friday. Barbo does not elaborate on the third step, contemplative prayer, which he says is ineffable.

In drawing up this work, Barbo was influenced in particular by a work of a Franciscan, Ubertino da Casale. Certainly Barbo's work also has much in common with the Flemish *devotio moderna,* represented by the *Imitation of Christ,* although the lines that connect him with the movement are not clear. In adopting this methodical form of prayer, Barbo was drawing on the most successful spiritual movement of his times, even if later centuries of Benedictines chafed at the idea of the introduction of this alien form of meditation, which seemed to distance prayer too much from the liturgical life of the monks.

Barbo, then, was not afraid to adopt some fairly drastic innovations in polity and piety in order to breathe new life into monasteries, where the fire of divine love and Christian service was burning very low.

BEDE (CA. 673–735)

Saint Bede, who is also called Bede the Venerable, was a teacher, historian, and biblical interpreter. He was born on lands belonging to the monks of the Northumbrian abbey of Wearmouth, to whom he was confided when he was seven. Soon he moved to the monastic foundation at Jarrow, where he spent almost all of the rest of his life. He was ordained a deacon when he was nineteen and a priest when he was thirty. He wrote a much-used manual on calculating the time for Easter, commentaries on many books of the Bible, and several saints' lives. Perhaps he is best known today as the author of the *Ecclesiastical History of the English Nation.*

Bede lived during a period when monasteries often drew on several different written rules for their observances. Bede knew the *Rule of Benedict,* though his life was not governed by it exclusively. Bede was on friendly terms with bishops and monks elsewhere, some of whom helped him with his historical research. Largely through the efforts of his first abbot, Benet Biscop, Bede's own Northumbrian monastery had a fine library for those days. Bede had a solid knowledge of the teachings of the church, which he tried to pass on to the English clergy of his time. When he died, he was working on an English translation of the Gospel of John.

Bede's *Homilies on the Gospels,* which is quoted here, emphasizes exegesis and doctrine, not morality. Sometimes his sermons have two parts, one explaining the Gospel reading for a certain day, and the other explaining the feast being celebrated that day. They are lucid and not particularly long. Christ is the focus of Bede's expositions.

In 796 the twin abbeys of Wearmouth and Jarrow were destroyed by marauding Vikings. Vikings would continue to devastate England for more than a century. Then, in the tenth century, there was a strong rebirth of Benedictine monasticism in England under Dunstan (abbot of Glastonbury, then bishop of Worcester [957–959] and archbishop of Canterbury), Oswald (bishop of Worcester [961–992]), and Ethelwold (bishop of Winchester [963–984]). The customs inculcated by the reform were contained in the *Regularis concordia.* In the course of the reform, monastic influence in the English church increased significantly. King Edgar supported the reform—in part, perhaps, because he shared the reformers' belief that only such a reform would save England from divine punishment. Wulfstan of Worcester was the spiritual heir of these three restorers of English Christianity and English monasticism.

BENEDICT OF NURSIA (CA. 480–CA. 550)

What is known about Saint Benedict comes either from his *Rule* or from the second book of the *Dialogues* (593–594) of Pope Saint Gregory I (d. 604), which is primarily a collection of miracle stories. Gregory does give us a credible picture of Benedict as a monastic guide who combined austerity with gentleness in the same paradoxical mixture one finds in his *Rule.*

Benedict was born in Nursia, seventy miles north of Rome. His parents were probably provincial landowners. He was sent to be educated at Rome, but left the city because of the sinful atmosphere he found there. Around A.D. 500, he began to live as a hermit in a cave at Subiaco, fifty miles east of Rome. He was given provisions by the monk Romanus, who lived in a nearby monastery. After three years of solitude, Benedict was persuaded to become abbot of a monastery in the area. His tenure ended in failure when the monks tried to poison him. Gradually, a community formed around him at Subiaco, and he established a group of monasteries, perhaps on the Pachomian model. The jealousy of a local priest persuaded him to move on. With several disciples, he went next to Monte Cassino, a tall, sunbaked hill eighty miles south of Rome on a main highway—the Via Latina, between Rome and Naples. There he worked to convert the local people to the Christian faith and oversaw the growth of a single large monastery, for which he wrote his *Rule.* He was buried at Monte Cassino sometime around 550. Gregory tells us that Benedict sorrowfully foresaw the sacking of his monastery. The monastery was sacked and destroyed by the Lombards in 581, the surviving monks fleeing to Rome.

Benedict had experienced firsthand various forms of monastic life: solitary (also called eremitic), Pachomian (groupings of small, geographically proximate communities under a chain of command leading to an abbot in chief), and cenobitic (a single community under a single abbot). It was for the latter sort of independent community that he wrote what he called his "little rule" for beginners. His *Rule* drew on the monastic tradition as handed down by the desert fathers, whose sayings and lives were available in Latin. Benedict's *Rule* was also very indebted to Cassian, who traveled extensively in Egypt before bringing his reports on the teaching and practices of the Eastern monks to France. Finally, Benedict made use of the *Rule of the Master,* evidently the work of an Italian monk whose life overlapped with Benedict's. Benedict drew most of the prologue and first seven chapters of his *Rule* from this eccentric document, though he modified it profoundly, shortening it and making it seem much more reasonable, as least to most modern readers. Because we can compare the *Rule of the Master* with the *Rule of Benedict,* we have been able to learn much about Benedict's intentions—even in the unlikely event that Benedict himself wrote the *Rule of the Master* and later revised it to what we know as the *Rule of Benedict.*

Benedict's *Rule* summarizes the written records of more than two hundred years of monastic experience, as well as a lifetime of monastic searching on Benedict's part. The *Rule* is a very practical document. Apart from the prologue and parts of the first few chapters, Benedict's goal was to lay out a framework within which monks could live and pray and be schooled in the Lord's service. Theology and theory are never far below the surface, but the *Rule* looks primarily to conduct.

The usual day of Benedict's monks began at about 2 A.M. with the night office, or vigils. During the rest of the day there were seven additional offices, the most important of which were lauds and vespers, which the monasteries had adopted from the church at large. These eight offices (referred to in their entirety as the liturgy of the hours) were carefully constructed of traditional elements: psalms, biblical readings, antiphons, and some readings from Christian writers. The entire Psalter was recited once a week. On the average, Benedict's monks probably prayed the liturgy three and a half hours a day.

Work required some six and a half hours. For Benedict, to turn from prayer to work was not to turn from the supernatural to the mundane; work, too, was a holy service, not merely a hedge against idleness or a means of support. A third component of each day was holy reading *(lectio divina),* to which some four hours were devoted. This reading was more studious or theological than what has been known in recent times as spiritual reading, and more devout and religious than ordinary study. It was meant to form the monk's mind, imagination, and affectivity in the image of Christ. It was serious work: one was to read entire works, from beginning to end, in order, thoughtfully. It was also prayerful: one was to make the truth one's own, to savor it and learn it by heart.

The ordering of the day was not to be so rigidly construed that monks could not take time to help one another with tasks or problems when the occasion arose. Nor were the monks to be so preoccupied with their own concerns that they could not take time to welcome guests and travelers—who, Benedict said matter-of-factly, are never lacking in a monastery.

The whole of this monastic life was conducted in an atmosphere of quiet and reverence. Absolute silence and sign language were not part of Benedict's regime, though they were adopted later in some monasteries. Similarly, although Benedict liked order, the *Dialogues,* even if the picture Gregory presents there is not particularly accurate, reminds us that in Benedict's time, when rival popes and rival armies and races vied for ecclesiastical and political power, good order was not that of an eighteenth-century garden. Something similar can be said about enclosure. Benedict wanted monasteries to be self-sufficient, and he didn't want his monks wandering outside the monastery or gossiping about secular matters. However, he did build his monastery on a main highway and made provision for monks being sent out of the cloister on journeys both short and long.

Benedict's *Rule* provides for three promises: obedience, stability, and *conversatio morum.* Obedience is to the *Rule,* abbot, and community; stability is life in community under a rule and an abbot; and *conversatio morum* seems to mean something like "monastic lifestyle." In other words, the three promises seem to boil down to one: to embrace the monastic life in a particular community. Whatever community that might be, it would require dispossession of material goods (poverty) and chastity as part of monastic life. Even the monk's attachment to his community through the threefold promise was not absolute. A monk could grow in community in such a way that he was then called to live on his own as a hermit. He might also, it turned out, be sent to missions and other places that, ironically, were not necessarily more solitary than life in community. One thinks, for example, of the monk-missionaries and monk-bishops of the "Benedictine centuries" of the early Middle Ages, men and women like Boniface and Walburga, missionaries to Germany, and Wulfstan of Worcester.

BERNARD OF CLAIRVAUX (1090–1153)

By the end of the eleventh century, the Benedictine rule and tradition no longer enjoyed the same monopoly they had hitherto held among celibate Christian communities in Europe. A first step toward this multiplicity of rules was represented by the Cistercians. The first Cistercian abbey, Cîteaux, was founded in France in 1098 by Saint Robert of Molesme, Saint Stephen Harding, and others who wished to live a secluded life more literally patterned on the *Rule of Benedict,* yet went on to create their own distinct order. Born of noble family, Bernard entered Cîteaux in 1112. In 1115 he was sent to be founding abbot of Clairvaux. Bernard soon became one of the most powerful people in Europe. He helped the Knights Templar receive ecclesiastical approbation; he championed Innocent II against an antipope; he wrote a treatise, *On Consideration,* for Pope Eugene III, who had been a monk at Clairvaux; he preached against heretics and on behalf of the Second Crusade. He was instrumental in the condemnation of some of the teachings of Peter Abelard and Bishop Gilbert de la Porré.

Bernard was a brilliant writer. His liturgical sermons are moving still. His eighty-six sermons on the Song of Songs are one of the masterpieces of European literature. In these allegorical readings of the Song of Songs, he ranges from the most pedestrian concerns of monastic life to the heights of contemplation. His book *On the Love of God* argues that God should be loved simply because God is God. His treatise *On the Stages of Humility and Pride* is a masterpiece of psychological analysis and irony. In this work Bernard avoids discussing the stages of humility outlined in the *Rule of Benedict,* purportedly because he knows more about pride than humility, and devotes himself instead to a penetrating study of pride.

LOUIS DE BLOIS (1506–1566)

In 1520, at the age of fourteen, Louis de Blois (Blosius) entered the Benedictine monastery of Liessies in Hainaut. The abbot at that time was eager to improve the life of the community. He confided Louis's training to a novice master who shared his desire for monastic restoration. Louis was sent to Ghent (1522–1524) and then to the University of Louvain, where he studied Latin, Greek, and Hebrew and earned his licentiate in arts in 1527. That same year, at the age of twenty-two, Louis was elected coadjutor abbot. He continued his studies in theology at Louvain until he succeeded to the abbacy in 1530.

Louis immediately began to teach his monks by word and example. He wrote his *Speculum monachorum* (*Mirror for Monks,* 1538) to teach his monks the love of prayer and religious virtues. When war threatened between Francis I and Charles V, Louis and three other religious took refuge on some monastery property in a small village. There they lived an exemplary religious life, which drew others to join them. At the urging of the community at Liessies, he returned there. He wrote up a set of *statuta* or customs (*Statuta monastica,* 1539). Blosius was instrumental in the installation of the recently founded Jesuits at Louvain. He himself made the retreat prescribed in the *Exercises of Saint Ignatius* and later required all postulants to the monastery to have made the same retreat.

In a series of treatises Blosius spelled out his spiritual doctrine: *Rule of Spiritual Life* (*Canon vitae spiritualis*), *Collection of Devout Prayers* (*Piarum precularum cimeliarchion*), *Manual for the Humble* (*Enchiridion parvulorum*), *Recreation for the Soul* (*Psychagogia*). He began a second series of works with the *Spiritual Doctrine* (1551). This series he concluded with a four-part book, the most important part of which was the *Spiritual*

Mirror (Speculum spirituale). Blosius's works were translated many times into most European languages and exercised a considerable influence on Catholic spirituality.

Much of this voluminous spiritual writing consists of extracts from other authors, the fruit of Louis's reading and meditation. Although he was open to many influences, his spirituality is thoroughly Benedictine. His sources are the Bible, the early Christian writers, the monastic authors, and the liturgy. He frequently cites the works of the Rhineland mystics: Suso, Tauler, and Ruusbroeck, as well as Gertrude, Mechthild, Birgitta, and Catherine of Siena. In his writings, the twin currents of Rhineland mysticism and *Devotio moderna* flow together into a synthesis rooted in the Benedictine tradition.

Blosius's goal is practical, his style simple and direct. He is psychologically astute, kind, and positive. The love of Christ is the motive and the goal. He is particularly devoted to Christ in his sufferings, which he regards as the royal road to human beings' union with the divinity. He describes this union in traditional terms: the believer is joined to God without an intermediary and becomes one spirit with God; the believer is plunged into God like iron into fire. Blosius lived to see the beginnings of the Reformation and even wrote a book directed at heretics *(Collyre hereticorum).*

SR. JOAN CHITTISTER (B. 1936)

A vigorous social activist, writer, and Benedictine monastic who believes that monastics, like all Christians, should be involved in the struggle for social justice, Sr. Joan Chittister, O.S.B., is a member and former prioress of Mount Saint Benedict Monastery in Erie, Pennsylvania. She holds a graduate degree from the University of Notre Dame and a Ph.D. in speech communication theory from Pennsylvania State University. She has served as president of the Congregation of Saint Scholastica, president of the Conference of American Benedictine Prioresses, and a U.S. delegate to the International Union of Superiors General, and she is a past president of the Leadership Conference of Women Religious, where she has also served as chairperson of the LCWR National Task Force on Peacemaking. She is a columnist for the *National Catholic Reporter.* She received an award from *U.S. Catholic* magazine in 1992 for her work for justice, peace, and equality in church and society. In addition to her studies of Benedictine spirituality, she has written many other books and articles. Some of her recent titles include *A Passion for Life: The Face of God* (with Robert Lenz; 1996), *The Fire in These: A Spirituality of Contemporary Religious Life* (1995), and *There Is a Season* (with John August Swanson; 1996). She has frequent speaking engagements throughout North America.

THE DESERT FATHERS AND MOTHERS

In addition to Pachomius and Antony, there were thousands of monks in Egypt and Palestine, most of whose names have not survived. Particularly among the monks of Egypt there developed a body of proverbial sayings and stories. These were passed on by word of mouth and then by writing. Through these written sayings collections, through the lives of monks like Antony and Pachomius, and through reports of those who went out to the desert to visit the monks, the teachings of these men and women who sought obscurity in the desert continue to fascinate and teach today. Helen Waddell, Thomas Merton, and Benedicta Ward have all taken a hand at translating these sayings.

Like Mother Teresa or Dorothy Day, the desert *abbas* and *ammas* embraced a radical sort of Christianity, which sought to strip individuals of anything that would stand between them and their God. Saint Jerome (ca. 345–420), who was the associate and propagandist of the desert monks, summed up their goal: "naked to follow the naked Christ." Like the Cynics, they wanted to be free. Unlike the Cynics, they found their freedom in a society of their own making. They built up the forms of that society by trial and error. What they learned from their successes and failures on their quest for freedom to be with God they handed on in stories and sayings, which, like Jesus' parables and the Zen masters' koans, are meant to tease the mind of the hearers to see truths long overlooked. Through them we can glimpse the lives of the desert monks, but the primary purpose of these sayings is to teach practical wisdom, not record historical fact. The sayings of the desert monks seldom touch on mystical experiences.

When these sayings and stories were written down, they were arranged either alphabetically under the names of well-known monks, or by themes in what are called *systematic collections*. Some sayings never found their way into either sort of arrangement. The sayings do not provide techniques for self-control or ecstasy or union with God. There was no single theory or method of spirituality in the desert, only the haphazardly accumulated wisdom of thousands of devout Christians following a difficult calling in which they waited humbly, longingly, and contritely for the transforming grace of God.

ESTHER DE WAAL (B. 1930)

Esther de Waal is an Anglican woman who, though not herself a nun, has become an articulate spokesperson of monastic tradition and values. She spent her childhood in a country vicarage on the Welsh border. She studied history at Cambridge University, did research as an associate of the Department of Local History at Leicester University, and became research fellow and college lecturer at Newnham. She married Victor de Waal in 1960. She then taught in Cambridge and Nottingham before moving to Lincoln, where her husband was chancellor of Lincoln Cathedral and she a member of the staff of Lincoln Theological College. She also taught for the Open University. Later the family moved to Canterbury and she found herself, as the wife of the Anglican dean of Canterbury, living in the prior's house of the former monastery. There she raised her four sons while continuing to teach.

She began exploring Benedictine tradition and spirituality. In 1982 she launched a program called "Benedictine Experience," in which a group of Americans lived at Canterbury for ten days and followed a modified Benedictine regime. In 1984 she published *Seeking God: The Way of Saint Benedict* (1985). She followed this with *Living with Contradiction: Further Reflections on the Rule of Saint Benedict* (1989). Esther de Waal also has lectured widely on Benedictine spirituality.

Returning to live in the country, she published *A Life-Giving Way: A Commentary on the Rule of Saint Benedict* (1995), which is a chapter-by-chapter commentary on the *Rule of Benedict*. Her commentary is informed by the latest scholarship, but it is also the product of years of practice in Benedictine spirituality. Her gentle wisdom is everywhere evident in her interpretations and applications of Benedict's words. In 1993 she published *A Seven Day Journey with Thomas Merton*. More recently, stimulated by worshiping in the former church of Dore Abbey, a Cistercian monastery near her home, she has produced a study of Cistercian spirituality: *The Way of Simplicity: The Cistercian Tradition* (1998). Another, related interest of de Waal's is Celtic spirituality. She edited *God under My Roof: Celtic Songs and Blessings* (1984) and *The Celtic Vision* (1990), and she wrote *The Celtic Way of Prayer* (1997).

GERTRUDE THE GREAT (1256–CA. 1302)

In 1220, a group of seven nuns set out from Halberstadt to found a new monastery. They had to move twice, in 1234 and 1258, before they found, at Helfta, the site they were looking for. Even after this last move, to a quiet valley in Saxony, the new foundation had a stormy history. It was pillaged in 1285, placed under interdict around 1295, destroyed in 1342, and restored in 1346. In its first hundred years, the community was home to a remarkable group of women who were contemporaries of Dante, Meister Eckhart, and Duns Scotus.

The first of these was Abbess Gertrude of Hackeborn, who began her forty-year term of office in 1251. Ten years later she received into the community a four-year-old namesake, later to be known as Gertrude the Great. This younger Gertrude received an excellent education in the convent. When she was twenty-five she had a profound conversion experience. From then on her intellectual activity centered on theology. Although she was never physically strong, she wrote two works in Latin, *The Herald of Divine Love* and *The Spiritual Exercises*. *The Herald of Divine Love* has five parts: the first is her biography, written by some else; the second is directly from her hand; the third, fourth, and fifth were composed by one of her fellow sisters from her teachings. Other outstanding members of the monastery at Helfta included the abbess's blood sister, Mechthild of Hackeborn (1241/42–1298/99), and Mechthild of Magdeburg (1207–1282/94).

The life of Gertrude the Great and the lives of the rest of the community at Helfta centered on the liturgy. Most of Gertrude's two works are closely connected with the feasts of the liturgical year and the hours of the liturgical office. In this, of course, Gertrude is representative of medieval monastics, for whom the rhythms of the liturgical seasons and the succession of the hours divided time into sacred seasons and hours. As one might expect of someone who drew the sustenance of her spiritual life from the liturgy, Gertrude's writings are saturated with scriptural words and ideas. Christ is at the center of her spirituality. She and her collaborators were good Latin stylists. Nevertheless, her writings can be off-putting to modern readers, but once one becomes familiar with her style, one can be inspired by reading the thoughts of someone who drew from the Bible and the liturgy direction and zeal to devote every ounce of her strength to praising God and finding ways to effectively love her fellow human beings.

HILDEGARD OF BINGEN (1098–1179)

Hildegard of Bingen was born in 1098, the tenth child of a noble family. In 1106 or 1108 she was sent to be raised by the noble lady Jutta, who was an *inclusa* (a hermit who lived in a cell attached to a church). Jutta was attached to the monastery of Benedictine men at Disibodenberg in the Rhineland. Gradually her hermit's cell grew to be a small community of women. Jutta was evidently teacher and guide to these women. Hildegard later declared that from the time she was a little girl she experienced visions but for many years was afraid to tell anyone about them. Hildegard seems to have pronounced vows as a Benedictine in this community about 1112–1115. During her years under Jutta, she must have learned a great deal, from Jutta herself, from participation in the liturgy, and perhaps from personal study. However, Hildegard always maintained that her own learning was negligible and her wisdom divinely given.

In 1136 Hildegard became abbess of the nuns' community. In 1141 she had a vision commanding her to write down the theological teaching of her visions. She reluctantly undertook this task with the help of the monk Volmar, who remained her secretary until a year before she died. She was also assisted by a younger nun named Richardis, who later became an abbess elsewhere, much to Hildegard's dismay. For ten years (1141–1151) Hildegard worked on her comprehensive presentation of Christian faith and practice called the *Scivias*. She felt God wanted her to write it, but just to be sure, in 1148 she also consulted Bernard of Clairvaux and Pope Eugene III for their advice and approval. The *Scivias* (the title means "know the ways [of the Lord]") describes twenty-six visions, and ends with a version of her musical morality play, the *Ordo virtutum*.

In 1150 Hildegard and about twenty nuns moved to the Rupertsberg, near Bingen, to establish an independent monastery. This caused considerable conflict with the monks of Disibodenberg, who did not want to lose their sisters, in part because of the fame that Hildegard was attracting, and in part because of the financial losses to the men's community the departure of the women would involve. Today there are few traces of the Rupertsberg monastery. However, a second foundation at Eibingen (ca. 1165) is thriving, not far from the place where Hildegard built her second monastery. Hildegard wrote the lives of two seventh-century saints: Disibod, an Irishman who was the patron of Disibodenberg; and Rupert, the patron of the monastery she founded.

Amid the poverty and struggles of her new monastic home, Hildegard began her second major work: the *Book of Life's Merits* (1158–1163), which focuses on the conflict between virtue and vice in human history and human life. Meanwhile, she received many visitors who came to her for advice or healing. She wrote music, primarily for the liturgy, containing haunting monophonic melodies with highly compressed poetic texts. She carried on a voluminous correspondence with people who sought her advice, and with others, mainly prelates, for whom she volunteered advice and correction. She also became expert in natural history. She completed a final major work, the *Book of Divine Works*, which like the *Scivias* contains explanations of her visions.

Around 1158–1161, Hildegard made the first of four preaching tours that took her to Mainz, Würzburg, Bamberg, Trier, Metz, Andernach, Cologne, Maulbron, and Hirsau. The last years of her life were embroiled in a fight with the church officials of Mainz regarding the burial of an excommunicated man. Eventually, Hildegard and her community were exonerated.

Before her death in 1179, her *Vita* was begun by a monk named Gottfried; it was finished after her death by another monk, Theoderich. The process for her canonization was never finished, but she is venerated as a saint locally and in the Benedictine order. She was one of most remarkable women of the Middle Ages, a genius in many fields, and a saintly Benedictine.

HUGH OF CLUNY (1024–1109)

Hugh was born of a noble Burgundian family and entered the monastery of Cluny when he was fourteen, after overcoming his father's opposition. He was appointed prior (second in command) before he was twenty-one, and in 1049 he succeeded Abbot Odilo. During his sixty years as abbot, Hugh was the advisor to nine popes and had great influence in affairs of church and state. He supported the reform efforts of Pope Gregory VII and sought to reconcile him with Emperor Henry IV. In 1095 he witnessed the consecration of a new church at Cluny; it was then the largest church in Christendom.

Hugh was noteworthy for his ability to combine deep piety with administrative effectiveness. An early biography of Hugh says that his physical bearing and appearance displayed outwardly his inner harmony. His presence was inspiring to those who knew him. He was very devoted to prayer and reading. It seemed that when he was reading, God spoke to him in a palpable way, and that when he prayed he spoke face-to-face with God. He practiced stern asceticism, but was not so demanding of others. He was a monk through and through.

JEAN MABILLON (1632–1707)

Jean Mabillon received his early education from his uncle, a priest, then studied at the university and the seminary at Reims. In 1653 he entered the monastery of Saint Remi in Reims. Saint Remi belonged to the Benedictine Congregation of Saint Maur, or Maurists, which had a centralized organization and emphasized scholarship. Shortly after making his monastic vows in 1654, he began to suffer from acute headaches brought on by his intense studies. He was sent to the monastery of Corbie and ordained a priest in 1660. He was cured of his headaches through the intercession of Saint Adalard, the founder of Corbie. In 1663 he went to Saint Denis, where he worked on a revision of the edition of the works of Bernard of Clairvaux. In 1664 he became assistant to Dom Luc d'Achéry, the librarian at Saint-Germain-des-Prés, who was working on the *Acta Sanctorum OSB (Acts of Benedictine Saints)*. There Mabillon spent the rest of his life completing the two works mentioned and producing an important study of paleography and manuscript studies entitled *De re diplomatica* (1691) and other learned works. He trained a generation of young scholars and traveled throughout Europe studying manuscripts.

Mabillon found a worthy adversary in Armand-Jean le Bouthillier de Rancé (1626–1700), a distinguished classical scholar, a graduate of the Sorbonne, and the abbot of the Cistercian abbey of La Trappe. In 1683 Abbot de Rancé wrote a work entitled *On the Holiness and Duties of the Monastic Life*. With reference to this work, Mabillon wrote a book explaining the Maurist commitment to study. His work provoked an impassioned reply from de Rancé. Mabillon did not reply immediately, but let his thoughts on the subject mature. Then in 1691 he published his *Traité des études monastiques (Treatise on the Studies of Monks)*. The work is divided into three parts. In the first, Mabillon argues that monastic discipline cannot flourish in monasteries where study is neglected; in the second, Mabillon discusses which studies are most suited to monks; in the third, he focuses on the purpose of monastic studies. After a further written exchange, Mabillon and de Rancé met and agreed to end the controversy.

Mabillon held that the most important studies for monks are those that form in them the new man, of which Christ was the model. He cautioned against vanity and pride—which, he said, will be avoided if monks' studies help them to know themselves in order to become more humble and to know, love, and serve God more perfectly. A few days before his own death, Mabillon advised a young priest: "Be true in everything. Be scrupulously sincere."

Mabillon was brilliant but modest. He was a humble servant of truth. His example, as much as his writings, shows the compatibility of the monastic vocation with scholarship. He was the embodiment of the ideals of the Maurist Congregation, to which belonged many French monasteries in the seventeenth and eighteenth centuries.

THOMAS MERTON (1915–1968)

Thomas Merton is the most important monastic writer of the twentieth century. He was not a great speculative theologian or biblical scholar; he may never be canonized; he may have written too much. Nevertheless, he was a brilliant writer with an incisive mind, a courageous man whose words lodged in the hearts of millions of readers.

Thomas Merton's father was born in New Zealand, his mother in Ohio. They were artists and lived in London, France, and New York. Merton's mother died when he was six, and his father spent much of the next decade in France. Thomas Merton attended a boarding school in England (his father died when he was sixteen), then enrolled at Cambridge. After a disastrous year there, he transferred to Columbia University, where he converted to Catholicism in 1938. At Columbia he deepened his knowledge of English literature and became friends with exponents of neoscholastic philosophy; he received his M.A. in 1939. In December 1941 he entered the Trappist Abbey of Gethsemani in Kentucky. He was to remain a member of the abbey until the day he died, though in his later years he had voiced many questions about the Trappists' way of life.

Early in his life at Gethsemani, he was very happy. His enthusiastic embrace of Trappist life is evident in his autobiography, *The Seven Storey Mountain* (1948). He was ordained a priest in 1949. In the next few years he published *The Waters of Siloe* (1950), *Ascent to Truth* (1952), and *Bread in the Wilderness* (1953). In a telling and true statement, Merton told Mark Van Doren, who had remarked that he

hadn't changed much, "Why should I? Here our duty is to become more ourselves, not less." His growing longing for solitude was expressed in some notes,
published five years after he wrote them, called *Thoughts in Solitude* (1958).

He was appointed novice master in the same year that saw the publication of
No Man Is an Island (1955). With this book Merton seems to have become more
open to the intellectual world around him, more willing to bring contemporary
experience and living tradition into dialogue. No longer so inclined to teach as to
question, he recorded his thinking during this time in *Conjectures of a Guilty Bystander,* which, though not published until 1966, contains writings from 1956 onward. Merton in effect accuses himself of having been a bystander. From now on
he will grapple with the issues of his contemporaries. As he said in *Thoughts in Solitude,* genuine solitude brings not separation but solidarity. Merton already was ex-
changing letters with many people, but from about 1958 onward he initiated new
contacts. In his writings he began to deal with issues like the Vietnam War, racial
discrimination, and poverty. He was finally allowed his hermitage on the grounds
of the Abbey of Gethsemani. Tragically, Merton was accidentally killed while at-
tending an international meeting in Bangkok in 1968.

PACHOMIUS (CA. A.D. 292–346)

Pachomius was one of the greatest monastic leaders of all time, a skilled organizer
and a skilled reader of the human heart. We know of him through several versions
of his life and through sermons and legislation attributed to him. The best source
about him seems to be a document called *The First Greek Life*. According to this
document, Pachomius, born about A.D. 292, probably in upper Egypt, was impressed into the army about 312. He and his fellow conscripts were taken to
Thebes, where some Christians, taking pity on their distress, brought them something to eat and drink. Pachomius prayed to God that if God would deliver him, he
would serve God all his life, loving all men and helping them according to God's
command. When he was discharged, Pachomius went to the Upper Thebaid, accepted baptism at Chenoboskion, and began serving the poor.

Pachomius became an anchorite under the guidance of a monk named
Palamon, who at first put him off. Together they practiced asceticism and prayed.
They spun and wove hair sacks to support themselves and to provide for the poor.
Pachomius sought to guard his heart from evil influences. He learned the Scriptures by heart. One day a voice reminded him of his promise to "reconcile hu-
mankind with God." Some time later he was traveling through the desert and came
to a deserted village called Tabennesi. A voice told him to build a monastery there,
for many were going to come there to become monks. Pachomius discerned the
will of God in what the voice told him. He and his brother John set about building
a monastery. Others began to arrive. Pachomius taught them by his example of
serving others, but many took advantage of him. Eventually, he was forced to insist
on obedience to his commands and to expel those who wouldn't listen. Whatever
rules he did establish were secondary; the Scriptures were the primary rule.

Pachomius organized the community quite carefully, appointing officials and
distributing tasks. The *koinonia* (community as a whole) was headed by Pachomius

and his successors; the local communities were guided by a "senior" or "father," each of whom had a second-in-command; the houses into which the local community was divided were governed by a housemaster and his second. Pachomius incorporated other monasteries into his network. There was a general meeting twice annually.

Pachomius built a monastery for his sister and other women who might join her. He appointed the monk Peter to guide them and sent brothers to help the nuns with buildings, burials, and other tasks. Pachomius worked many miracles in imitation of the Lord, but he was not dismayed when his prayers were not answered.

All his life, he preferred to teach by example rather than by rules. Whatever rules he laid down he lived himself. In 328 a teenager named Theodore arrived at the monastery, whom Pachomius groomed to exercise authority as he himself exercised it. Theodore was charming and proved an able assistant to Pachomius, but Pachomius had to work hard to soften Theodore's tendency to be too strict and austere. His relationship with Theodore was fairly stormy.

In grooming Theodore to be his successor, Pachomius sought to provide for a smooth transition after his death. In the event, however, Pachomius was succeeded first by Petronius, who died almost immediately; then by Horsiesios (346–350); only then by Theodore (350–368); and finally once again by Horsiesios.

PETER OF CELLE (CA. 1115–1183)

Peter was born at Aunoy-les-Minimes near Provins. His family was of the lesser nobility of Champagne. He evidently studied in Paris, perhaps while living at the monastery of Saint Martin des Champs. We find him next at the abbey of Montier-la-Celle, where he became abbot. He was evidently an energetic abbot. He supported Alexander III against an antipope and wrote letters of friendship or admonition to various monasteries. In 1161 Peter became abbot of the great abbey of Saint Remi at Reims. In that capacity he served as vicar general to his friend Archbishop Henry. This involved him in many legal matters, both civil and ecclesiastical. He corresponded with Alexander III and even admonished him. The pope in turn entrusted Peter with mandates to settle disputes and effect reforms.

Peter was a close friend of the brothers John and Richard of Salisbury. John had visited with Peter at Montier-la-Celle and dedicated the *Policraticus* to him. When John went into exile in 1163, he accepted Peter's invitation to stay at Saint Remi. His brother Richard also was sent into exile and stayed at Reims. Richard later became a canon regular at Merton in England. In 1179, Peter dedicated *The School of the Cloister* to Richard. In his last days as abbot, Peter oversaw the remodeling of the abbey church.

In 1178 Peter was on a list of possible cardinals, but the honor was not given him. In 1181, when John of Salisbury died as bishop of Chartres, Peter was appointed to succeed him. Peter died after only a few weeks as bishop.

Peter was a devout monk. He was devoted to Christ, especially in his sufferings and in the Eucharist. He was a excellent letter writer who corresponded widely. His letters are models of the mystique of friendship that flourished in the twelfth century. His correspondents are mainly ecclesiastics. Peter was friendly to members of all the emerging religious orders. He loved the church and was particularly concerned that the clergy be above reproach.

Peter's surviving writings include 175 letters and 96 sermons. Peter's sermons are centered on the liturgy; almost all of them deal with liturgical feasts. The sermon format seems to bring out the best in Peter. Amid his exuberant imagery, his sincerity and intelligence are evident and effective.

Peter also wrote five biblical works: two commentaries on Exodus 25–28, two treatises on the tabernacle, and a treatise on the various kinds of bread mentioned in the Bible. He also composed four treatises touching on the monastic life: *On the Purity of the Soul, On Affliction and Reading, On Conscience,* and, most important, *The School of the Cloister,* which is a thorough discussion of the disciplines of life in the cloister.

In *The School of the Cloister,* Peter gives several lists of the essential elements of cloistered (monastic) life. These lists include all the topics identified in this book except work and hospitality. It is interesting to ponder why Peter left these two out, since he was clearly a hard-working and hospitable man. It may also be that he regarded both activities as intruding on the austere ideas of withdrawal and contemplative prayer, which he seemed somewhat more eager to promulgate than to live.

SYNCLETICA (FL. CA. A.D. 400)

Among the sayings of the deserts fathers *(abbas)* are a few sayings of the desert mothers *(ammas).* Several dozen sayings survive from Amma Syncletica, all of them found also in the *Life of Syncletica,* which provides some basic information about Syncletica's life, though it is mainly about her teaching. We are told that Syncletica was a Macedonian whose ancestors had moved to Alexandria. Her family was well off and pious. She was beautiful and chaste, and, like one of her brothers, resistant to any family plans for her to marry. She was espoused to her beloved, Christ. While she was struggling to avoid being forced to marry, she became very thin. After her parents' death she was able to establish herself and her blind sister in the solitude of a relative's tomb. She gave all she had to the poor and had her hair cut off by priests. Then she devoted herself to a life of solitude, prayer, and fasting. She intensified her regimen when she was struggling against temptation, but moderated it at other times and so preserved her health.

Subsequently, like Saint Antony, she went further into solitude, but like him she was visited by those seeking advice and teaching. She would beg off, saying, "Why do you fantasize in this way about a sinner like me as if I were doing or saying something worthwhile? We have a common teacher—the Lord; we draw spiritual water from the same well and we suck our milk from the same breasts—the Old and the New Testaments." However, they persuaded her by their tears and arguments that it was her duty to instruct them. The majority of the *Life* is then devoted to her teaching. In the last years of her life she seems to have suffered from a hideous disease, probably cancer, which attacked first her lungs and then her mouth.

The Life of Syncletica tells us something of the monastic context of Syncletica's life, but gives us no information as to just when she lived. If indeed the teaching contained in that book is hers, then she must have lived during or after the lifetime of Evagrios of Pontus (346–399), whose teaching pervades the *Life*. Scholars believe the *Life* was written in the fifth century. It seems to come from a time before Evagrios's teaching had been condemned. In the introduction to her excellent translation, Elizabeth Bongie indicates that the *Life* itself had little influence. However, it seems to be a trustworthy witness to the monastic life of Syncletica's time.

Syncletica begins her teaching with a reference to the twofold law of love; this love is salvation. She then refers to the hundredfold, sixtyfold, and thirtyfold yield at harvest time, reserving the highest reward for consecrated virginity. However, she also reminds her audience of female monastics that women in the world may well "struggle more than we do." She distinguishes between those with a taste for contemplation and spiritual enlightenment, those inclined to asceticism, and those in the world who do good works.

The *Life* includes a treatise on chastity, which urges those committed to chastity not to run around unnecessarily, and to be careful in their speech and in their fantasies, and even in their relationships with other religious women. Evil fantasies should be driven out by other fantasies.

Next, she turns to poverty. Her doctrine is that radical divestment of ownership is good for those who have already practiced doing without. The devil is vanquished by poverty, because most sins have some relationship to possessions and their loss. Saying we must keep our "gain" hidden, Syncletica discusses humility at some length.

Then, turning to the Evagrian schema of "thoughts," Syncletica (or the author) warns first against feeling superior, which leads her to offer advice about how to deal with those who seem to be doing well and those who have fallen or are discouraged, which is elaborated in a teaching on pride and humility. There follows a very fine discussion of anger, which is explained to be an outward symptom of the very serious problem of remembering wrongs, from which flow envy, malicious talk, and sadness. There follows a very interesting and unusual section urging those who have been particularly gifted by grace to spend time in the company of abject sinners in order to help them.

The author spends a number of chapters warning against philosophical denials of free will. Origen was a vigorous defender of free will also, but one has the impression that this passage was prompted by a current controversy or danger. Then the author introduces some allegories that have the tone of pep talks, urging readers to stay the course. There follow some final exhortations regarding stability in community, the suitability of different persons for cenobitic or eremitic life, and the need for moderation and discretion.

Although the influence of Evagrios of Pontus is evident in the *Life,* the advice the book gives (and that is mostly what the *Life* does—give advice) seems rooted in experience and common sense. At crucial points the teaching invokes Christ as an example: his humility; his eating and spending time with sinners, which models the devout Christian's call to service of the abjectly wicked.

JOHN TRITHEMIUS (1462–1516)

John Trithemius was born at Trittenheim on the Moselle near Trier; hence the surname Trithemius. He studied at Trier, in the Low Countries, and at Heidelberg, but never earned a degree. In January 1482 he entered the monastery of Sponheim in the diocese of Mainz. He made profession as a Benedictine in November of the same year. Sponheim belonged to the reformed congregation of Bursfeld. In July 1483 Trithemius was elected abbot there, and was consecrated the following November. Both monastic reformer and humanist, he insisted on strict discipline while at the same time building up a renowned library of over two thousand manuscripts and books. Trithemius was in contact with many renowned scholars. He was forced to resign as abbot in 1506, whereupon he became abbot of the ancient Irish monastery of Saint Jakob in Würzburg. He died on December 13, 1516.

Although he did not have the benefit of a rigorous formal education, Trithemius had very broad interests and was an extremely learned man. He read widely in philosophy, studied Greek and Hebrew, and did reading and research in history and theology.

Trithemius was a prolific author. In 1513 he listed fifty-two works he had written; he composed another eight before he died. His works on church history include chronicles of Hirsau, Sponheim, and Saint Jakob of Würzburg. He also wrote a *De scriptoribus ecclesiasticis*. In several of these works, Trithemius seems to have padded his references with invented sources, but they have considerable value nevertheless. Trithemius also wrote many letters, a genre in which he excelled.

Of particular interest here are his ascetic works. He wrote a commentary on the prologue and first seven chapters of the *Rule of Benedict* entitled *On a Rule for the Those Living the Cloistered Life (De regimine claustralium)*. His other works include *On the Ruin of the Monastic Order (De ruina monastici ordinis)*, *On the Temptations of Religious (De religiosorum tentationibus)*, *On the Property of Monks (De proprietate monachorum)*, *On the Threefold Territory of Claustrals (De triplici regione claustralium)*. Among Trithemius's works are also versions of exhortations he gave to general chapters of the Bursfeld congregation and to his monks.

Summarizing a venerable idea of the Middle Ages as well as his own spiritual teaching, Trithemius declared in one of his letters: "Holy reading arouses the mind, meditation moves it to compunction; prayer seeks, contemplation finds." For Trithemius, study and monastic life lived for God were inseparable. The goal of study was to reach God himself. Study required asceticism, freedom from worldly cares. It was supposed to nourish the heart and draw it toward contemplation. Medieval monks had warned against *curiositas,* a craving for news and knowledge, which distracted one from seeking God. Trithemius used the same term, but with a different meaning: genuine study *(studiositas)* led to deeper knowledge and love of divine truth; vain learning *(curiositas)* sought to penetrate what is beyond the reach of the human mind. Like most monastic theorists before him, Trithemius felt that secular knowledge was not an end in itself, but only a means to help the monk study the Scriptures, which were the primary object of monastic study. Next in importance was the study of the early Christian writers. Trithemius distinguished intellectual or scholastic theology from affective or mystical theology, wherein love is primary and where the final point of arrival is the dark summit where divine truth dwells in inaccessible light.

WULFSTAN OF WORCESTER (CA. 1008–1095)

Saint Wulfstan's life was divided almost in half by the Norman invasion of England in 1066. He spent most of his life in the west Midlands of England, in the territory of the Severn River, which originates in Wales, flows east through Shrewsbury, then south to Worcester and the Bristol Channel. As bishop, Wulfstan came to know the area very well.

He was born at Itchington, near Warwick. His parents—Athelstan, a priest, and Wulfgiva—were fairly affluent. Wulfstan grew up during the Danish invasions. He was sent to Evesham Abbey for initial schooling, and soon afterward enrolled at the more distant abbey of Peterborough. Wulfstan returned home about 1024. In the next few years, his parents joined monasteries. We do not know what Wulfstan did between 1024 and 1034, when he entered the service of Bishop Brihtheah (1033–1038), who may have been his half-brother. Ordained a priest, Wulfstan performed his duties while devoting himself to fasting. After several years he asked permission to become a monk. Not long after his entry into the monastic community, Wulfstan was appointed successively novice-master and cantor. He increased his ascetic discipline by spending nights in prayer. Meanwhile, the see of Worcester passed to Bishop Lyfing, and then to Bishop Ealdred. Both were former abbots and busy men of affairs. By 1055 the latter had appointed Wulfstan prior. One of Wulfstan's main tasks was to recover those properties of the cathedral priory that had been unlawfully occupied by others. Wulfstan also sought to enhance the observance of the monks within the priory. In addition, he performed many pastoral functions on behalf of the bishop. He was particularly concerned that the laity know the tenets and obligations of their Christian faith. He earned the esteem of many, in particular Earl Harold Godwinson. In 1062, Wulfstan reluctantly agreed to become bishop of Worcester.

This position brought with it many new responsibilities both secular and ecclesiastical. However, throughout his years as bishop, Wulfstan tried to follow the monastic round of prayer. He devoted himself very zealously to his pastoral duties, preaching, consecrating churches, hearing confessions, and making visitations. When Edward died in January 1066, Wulfstan found himself confessor to the new king, Harold II. Within a year, William the Conqueror succeeded to the throne. Wulfstan advised people to submit to the new order.

His spiritual outlook was shaped by the monastic reform carried out in the mid–tenth century under Dunstan. Although Wulfstan remained loyal to this older English monastic reform movement, he was open to the monastic customs that Lanfranc, the first Norman archbishop of Canterbury and former teacher of Saint Anselm, brought from Normandy. Hence, politically and monastically he adapted to the new order. He remained in office under the Normans longer than any of the English bishops. He was humble and ready to serve wherever he was called. He gradually acquired a reputation as a holy man who could on occasion work miracles, especially on behalf of the sick. He was even-tempered and cheerful, but he insisted on a high level of religious observance among those of his household. He strongly opposed slavery and clerical marriage, while personally seeing to the care of the poor. He always remained an embodiment of the monastic ideals of his time, simplicity and purity of heart, which remained the foundation of his long pastoral career as a bishop.

The primary source for Wulfstan's life and character is William of Malmesbury's Latin *Life,* a reworking of a no longer extant English work by Wulfstan's close associate Coleman. All the stories about Wulfstan included in this book are from the Latin *Life.* There survives a book of prayers, the *Portifolium,* which the saint seems to have taken with him on his pastoral travels throughout his diocese.

Bibliographical Notes

ANSELM OF CANTERBURY

The works of Anselm of Canterbury are available in a six-volume critical Latin edition edited by F. S. Schmitt (Edinburgh: Nelson, 1946–1961). The *Memorials of St. Anselm,* ed. R. W. Southern and F. S. Schmitt, Auctores Britannici Medii Aevi, no. 1 (London: Oxford Univ. Press, 1969), shows his more familiar side.

An excellent study is R. W. Southern, *Saint Anselm: Portrait in a Landscape* (Cambridge: Cambridge Univ. Press, 1990). Benedicta Ward has published a convenient translation of Anselm's prayers, *The Prayers and Meditations of Saint Anselm* (New York: Penguin, 1973). The translations here are mine, from the critical edition.

ANTONY

The excerpts from Athanasius's *Life of Antony* are reworked from the annotated translation by Robert T. Meyer (Athanasius, *The Life of Saint Antony,* Ancient Christian Writers, no. 10 [Westminster, MD: Newman, 1950]). The translations of the letters are based on D. J. Chitty's translation (Oxford: Fairacres, 1975). A more recent edition of the letters can be found in Samuel Rubenson, *The Letters of St. Antony: Monasticism and the Making of a Saint* (Minneapolis: Fortress, 1995), from which work I derive some of my ideas about the relationship of Antony's very theologically informed letters to the picture of Antony presented in the *Life.* The *Sayings* of Antony I have translated primarily from *Les sentences des pères du désert: Collection alphabétique,* trans. Lucien Regnault (Sablé-sur-Sarthe: Abbaye Saint-Pierre de Solesmes, 1981). A more recent translation of the *Life* is Athanasius, *The Life of Antony and the Letter to Marcellinus,* trans. and ed. Robert C. Gregg, Classics of Western Spirituality (New York: Paulist Press, 1980).

LUDOVICO BARBO

The basics of Ludovico Barbo's life, reform, and writings, together with a bibliography, can be found in M. Mähler, "Barbo, Louis," in *Dictionnaire de spiritualité* (Paris: Beauchesne, 1937), 1:1244–1245; and in A. Pantoni, "Barbo, Ludovico," in *Dizionario degli Istituti di Perfezione* (Rome: Edizioni Paoline, 1974), 1:1044–1047. The most thorough study available to me was Ildefonso Tassi, *Ludovico Barbo (1381–1443),* Uomini e dottrine, no. 1 (Rome: Edizioni di Storia e Letteratura,

1952). Evidently wrong in its main contention about the Italian origin of the *Imitation of Christ,* but useful for its bibliography, is Riccardo Pitigliani, *Il Ven. Ludovico Barbo et la diffusione dell' Imitazione di Cristo per opera della Congregazione di S. Giustina* (Padua: Badia S. Giustina, 1943). Here selections from Barbo are translated from the Latin version of his directions for methodical prayer and meditation printed in Tassi, 141–152. Quotations from his letters are also translated from the Latin originals (Tassi, 152–155).

BEDE

Readers can find a first introduction to Saint Bede's life and works and the scholarship about him in the *Oxford Dictionary of the Christian Church,* 3rd ed., ed. F. L. Cross and E. A. Livingstone (New York: Oxford Univ. Press, 1997), 177–178; and Alberic Stacpole, "St. Bede," in *Benedict's Disciples,* ed. David Hugh Farmer (Leominster, England: Gracewing, 1997). Bede's homilies, edited by David Hurst, are to be found in *Bedae opera,* vol. 3/4, Corpus Christianorum, Series Latina, no. 122 (Turnhout, Belgium: Brepols, 1955). These were translated by Lawrence T. Martin and David Hurst as Bede the Venerable, *Homilies on the Gospels,* 2 vols., Cistercian Studies, nos. 110–111 (Kalamazoo, MI: Cistercian Publications, 1991). The translations here are my own.

BENEDICT OF NURSIA

The selections from the *Rule of Benedict* are translated from the Latin text prepared by Jean Neufville for the Sources chrétiennes series and reprinted in what is by far the best English-language commentary on the *Rule of Benedict:* Terrence G. Kardong, *Benedict's Rule: A Translation and Commentary* (Collegeville, MN: Liturgical Press, 1996). Still very useful is *RB 80: The Rule of St. Benedict in Latin and English with Notes* (Collegeville, MN: Liturgical Press, 1981). For Gregory's life of Benedict in the *Dialogues,* the best translation and commentary is Gregory the Great, *The Life of Saint Benedict,* commentary by Adalbert de Vogüé, trans. Hilary Costello and Eoin de Bhaldraithe (Petersham, MA: St. Bede's, 1993). The translation of passages from the *Dialogues* are my own. *The Rule of the Master* is available in an English translation by Luke Eberle (Kalamazoo, MI: Cistercian Publications, 1977).

BERNARD OF CLAIRVAUX

The works of Bernard of Clairvaux were published in a critical edition by Jean Leclercq, C. H. Talbot, and H. Rochais (Rome: Editiones Cistercienses, 1957–1977). They have been published in English translation by Cistercian Publications. I have translated from the Latin. English translations of the two works I have cited are Bernard of Clairvaux, *On the Song of Songs,* trans. Kilian Walsh and Irene Edmonds, 4 vols., Cistercian Fathers, nos. 4, 7, 31, and 40 (Kalamazoo, MI: Cistercian Publications, 1979–1983); and *On Consideration,* trans. Elizabeth Kennan and John D. Anderson, Cistercian Fathers, no. 37 (Kalamazoo, MI: Cistercian Publications, 1976). I have studied the latter in "The Spirituality of St. Bernard for Managers," *Cistercian Studies* 25 (1990): 267–276. There is an enormous amount of literature about Saint Bernard, much of it available from Cistercian Publications.

Various modern students of Saint Bernard, such as Brian Patrick McGuire, Jean Leclercq, Adriaan Bredero, and Michael Casey, have written studies and biographical sketches of Bernard, but there is really no standard or definitive work.

LOUIS DE BLOIS

Two years after Louis de Blois (Blosius) died, Jacques Froye edited his writings as *Ludovici Blosii opera* (Louvain, 1568); this collection went through eight editions. The monks of Liessies, under Abbot Antoine de Winghe, prepared a new edition (Anvers: Plantin, 1632), which was listed by Jean Mabillon in his *Traité des études monastiques* (1691). A good introduction to Louis de Blois can be found in P. de Puniet, "Blois, Louis de," in the *Dictionnaire de spiritualité* 1 (1937): 1730–1738. English versions of many of his works are to be found in *The Works of Louis de Blois*, ed. B. Wilberforce and D. R. Huddleston (London: Burns Oates and Washbourne, 1925–26). Up-to-date bibliography can be found in Lambert Vos, *Louis de Blois, Abbé de Liessies (1506–1566): Recherches bibliographiques sur son oeuvre*, Publications de l'Encyclopédie bénédictine, no. 1 (Turnhout, Belgium: Brepols, 1992). I have translated the quotations from the *Mirror for Monks (Speculum monachorum), Spiritual Doctrine (Institutionis spiritualis),* and the *Spiritual Mirror (Speculum spirituale)* from the *Opera omnia* of 1672 (Kempten: Rudolphe Dreber), which reprints the 1632 edition, and the quotations from his *Statuta monastica (Monatic Statutes)* from the edition that constituted the tenth volume in the series Scripta Monastica, ed. Ursmarus Berlière (Padua: Antoniana, 1929). I was unable to consult George de Blois, *A Benedictine of the Sixteenth Century* (London: Burns and Oates, 1878; translated from the original French edition [Paris, 1875]).

SR. JOAN CHITTISTER

Passages quoted from Joan Chittister are from *The Rule of Benedict: Insights for the Ages* (New York: Crossroad, 1996). A related book by Chittister is *Wisdom Distilled from the Daily: Living the Rule of St. Benedict Today* (San Francisco: HarperSanFrancisco, 1991).

THE DESERT FATHERS AND MOTHERS

The quotations from *Sayings of the Desert Fathers and Mothers* are my translations, taken primarily from *Les sentences des Pères du Désert: Série des anonymes,* Spiritualité Orientale, no. 43 (Bégrolles-en-Mauges: Abbaye de Bellefontaine, 1985), although I made use of other versions as well. For the English reader there are a number of translations available: Benedicta Ward, trans., *The Wisdom of the Desert Fathers: Systematic Sayings from the Anonymous Series of the Apophthegmata Patrum* (Oxford: SGL Press, 1986) and *The Sayings of the Desert Fathers: The Alphabetical Collection* (Kalamazoo, MI: Cistercian Publications, 1984); Thomas Merton, *The Wisdom of the Desert* (New York: New Directions, 1970); Helen Waddell, *The Desert Fathers* (1936; reprint, Ann Arbor: Univ. of Michigan Press, 1971).

ESTHER DE WAAL

Selections from Esther de Waal are taken from *A Life-Giving Way: A Commentary on the Rule of St. Benedict* (Collegeville, MN: Liturgical Press, 1995). De Waal also wrote two outstanding books on Benedictine spirituality: *Seeking God: The Way of*

St. Benedict (Collegeville, MN: Liturgical Press, 1984) and *Living with Contradiction* (Harrisburg, PA: Morehouse, 1998).

GERTRUDE THE GREAT

Passages from the first two books of *The Herald of Divine Love* are here translated from the critical edition of the Latin text, in Gertrude d'Helfta, *Oeuvres spirituelles,* vol. 2, *Le héraut,* books 1–2, ed. and trans. Pierre Doyère, Sources chrétiennes, no. 139 (Paris: Cerf, 1968). There is also a useful French version of the *Herald* by the nuns of Notre-Dame of Wisques, *Le héraut de l'amour divin: Révélations de Sainte Gertrude,* new ed., 2 vols. (Tours: Mame, 1952), from which a citation from book 5 is translated. There are two recent, though partial, English translations of this work: *The Herald of God's Loving-Kindness, Books One and Two,* trans. Alexandra Barrat (Kalamazoo, MI: Cistercian Publications, 1991); and *The Herald of Divine Love,* trans. Margaret Winkworth (New York: Paulist Press, 1993). Included here also are some passages from Gertrude's *Spiritual Exercises,* translated from the Latin text in *Oeuvres spirituelles,* vol. 1, *Les exercices,* ed. and trans. Jacques Hourlier and Albert Schmitt, Sources chrétiennes, no. 127 (Paris: Cerf, 1967). For an English translation, see *Spiritual Exercises,* ed. Gertrud Lewis and Jack Lewis (Kalamazoo, MI: Cistercian Publications, 1989). Sister Mary Jeremy, O.P., *Scholars and Mystics* (Chicago: Regnery, 1962), tells about the mystics of Helfta, and Cipriano Vagaggini, *Theological Dimensions of the Liturgy* (Collegeville, MN: Liturgical Press, 1977), 740–803, examines Gertrude's spirituality.

HILDEGARD OF BINGEN

Most of the passages from Hildegard of Bingen included here are from her *Liber vitae meritorum,* ed. Angela Carlevaris, O.S.B., Corpus Christianorum, Continuatio Mediaevalis, no. 90 (Turnhout, Belgium: Brepols, 1995). There is a complete English version: *The Book of the Rewards of Life,* trans. Bruce Hozeski (1994; reprint, New York: Oxford Univ. Press, 1997). A few passages are taken from her *Explanation of the Rule of Benedict,* ed. and trans. Hugh Feiss (Toronto: Peregrina, 1990). Texts cited from Hildegard's musical morality play the *Ordo virtutum* are translated from the edition by Audrey Davidson (Kalamazoo, MI: Western Michigan Univ., 1985). The text of the *Ordo virtutum* is also available in both Latin and English on the liner notes to the recording made by Sequentia for Deutsche Harmonia Mundi (1982). Hildegard's life and works are presented in Sabina Flanagan, *Hildegard of Bingen, 1098–1179: A Visionary Life* (New York: Routledge, 1990). There is an excellent translation of the *Scivias* by Columba Hart and Jane Bishop (New York: Paulist Press, 1990). There are many audio recordings of her musical works; particularly noteworthy are those by Sequentia. A reliable version of her *Vita* is *The Life of Holy Hildegard,* trans. Hugh Feiss (Toronto: Peregrina, 1995). Most of the other English translations of her works are based on imperfect Latin editions or German translations, and should be used with caution.

HUGH OF CLUNY

The essential facts and bibliography regarding Hugh of Cluny can be found in F. L. Cross and E. A. Livingstone, eds., *Oxford Dictionary of the Christian Church,* 3d ed.

(New York: Oxford Univ. Press, 1997), p. 799. Further information is available in Noreen Hunt, *Cluny under Saint Hugh* (Notre Dame, IN: Univ. of Notre Dame Press, 1968). The biographical passages included here are my translations from materials contained in H. E. H. Cowdrey, "Memorials of Abbot Hugh of Cluny (1049–1109)," *Studii Gregoriani,* vol. 11 (Rome: Libreria Ateneo Salesiano, 1978), 13–175.

JEAN MABILLON

Basic information on Jean Mabillon's life and works can be found in the article by J.-P. Müller in *Dizionario degli Istituti di Perfezione* 5 (1978): 793–796, and in the entry by G.-M. Oury in *Dictionnaire de spiritualité* 10 (1977): 1–4. Selections from Mabillon's *Traité des études monastiques (Treatise on the Studies of Monks)* are translated from the Gregg Press reprint (Farnborough, England: Gregg Press, 1967) of the original 1691 edition. Regarding the Maurists, see the article by J. Houlier in *Dizionario degli Istituti di Perfezione* 5 (1978): 1082–1089.

THOMAS MERTON

Thomas Merton's writings on monasticism were collected in *Contemplation in a World of Action* (New York: Doubleday, 1971), which contains an excellent introduction by Merton's friend Jean Leclercq, O.S.B. I make use of material from this anthology, but Merton's overtly monastic writings are of limited use here. The rest of his writings—the vast majority—were designed to present what he had learned in the monastery to readers in other ways of life. Hence these other writings are more congruent with the aims of this book. In his earlier writings, Merton tended to emphasize the differences between monastics in their cloisters and the rest of humanity out in the world. In late 1950s he became more and more aware of the solidarity that united the monk with the rest of humanity. This new attitude is reflected both in his reworking of *Seeds of Contemplation* (1949) in *New Seeds of Contemplation* (1962; reprint, New York: New Directions, 1972), and in his *Conjectures of a Guilty Bystander* (1966; reprint, New York: Doubleday-Image, 1968), the latter containing reworked journal entries from 1956 onward. Merton was by then more certain about the questions than the answers and ready to enter into dialogue about his conjectures with all people of goodwill.

PACHOMIUS

The passages from *Life of Pachomius* are from "Pachomius: The First Greek Life," trans. Armand Veilleux, in *Pachomian Koinonia,* vol. 1, *The Life of Saint Pachomius* (Kalamazoo, MI: Cistercian Publications, 1980), 297–423. There is another version of this same *Life*, giving the critical Greek text: *The Life of Pachomius,* trans. Apostolos N. Athanassakis (Missoula, MT: Scholars Press, 1975). Most of the biography of Pachomius in the historical section is derived from this life. I also profited from some unpublished notes of Terrence Kardong, O.S.B., who followed another ancient version of Pachomius's life but drew from it substantially the same picture of Pachomius that I do. Fr. Kardong also discussed many of the same episodes quoted in the thematic section. For recent scholarly work, see Philip Rousseau, *Pachomius: The Making of a Community in Fourth-Century Egypt* (Berkeley: Univ. of California

Press, 1985); and Vincent Desprez, "Pachomian Cenobitism," *American Benedictine Review* 43 (1992): 233–249, 358–394.

PETER OF CELLE

The Latin texts of most of Peter of Celle's works are printed in volume 202 of J. P. Migne's *Patrologia latina*. Several works were edited by Jean Leclercq in his study *La spiritualité de Pierre de Celle,* Etudes de théologie et d'histoire de la spiritualité, no. 7 (Paris: J. Vrin, 1946). Gérard de Martel edited Peter's two commentaries on Ruth and Peter's treatise *De tabernaculo,* Corpus Christianorum, Continuatio Mediaevalis, no. 54 (Turnhout, Belgium: Brepols, 1983). English translations of *On Affliction and Reading, On Conscience, The School of the Cloister,* and sermons 29, 33, 39, and 44 appear in Peter of Celle, *Selected Works,* trans. Hugh Feiss, Cistercian Studies, no. 100 (Kalamazoo, MI: Cistercian Publications, 1987). All the passages included here are new translations from the Latin text in *L'école du cloître,* ed. and trans. Gérard de Martel, Sources chrétiennes, no. 240 (Paris: Cerf, 1977); or from the Latin text of *De afflictione et lectione* edited by Leclercq.

SYNCLETICA

The quotations from the *Life of Syncletica* were all transcribed (with minor alterations) from the translation by Elizabeth Bryson Bongie (Toronto: Peregrina, 1996). Other literature includes Elizabeth Castelli, "Pseudo-Athanasius: The Life and Activity of the Holy and Blessed Teacher Syncletica," in *Ascetic Behavior in Greco-Roman Antiquity: A Sourcebook,* ed. Vincent L. Wimbush (Minneapolis: Fortress, 1990), 265–311; Kevin Corrigan, "Syncletica and Macrina: Two Early Lives of Women Saints," *Vox Benedictina* 6, no. 3 (July 1989): 241–257; and Mary Forman, "Amma Syncletica: A Spirituality of Experience," *Vox Benedictina* 10, no. 2 (winter 1993): 199–237.

JOHN TRITHEMIUS

Sources of information about John Trithemius include the article on him by P. Séjourné in *Dictionnaire de théologie catholique* 15 (1950): 1862–1867; the article by Klaus Ganzer in *Dictionnaire de spiritualité* 15 (1991): 1325–1328; and N. L. Brann, *The Abbot Trithemius: The Renaissance of Monastic Humanism,* Studies in the History of Christian Thought, no. 24 (Leiden: Brill, 1981). Selections included in this book are translated from *Ioannis Trithemii Spanheimensis . . . Abbatis eruditissimi opera pia et spiritualia,* ed. Ioanne Busaeo (Mainz: J. Albini, 1610). Selections from *De regimine claustralium,* his commentary on the *Rule of Benedict,* are identified by the short title *Rule.* The monks of Assumption Abbey were kind enough to let me work from their copy of the *Opera* of Trithemius as well as from their copy of a 1672 version of the works of Louis de Blois.

WULFSTAN OF WORCESTER

All the selections about Wulfstan of Worcester are taken from *The Vita Wulfstani of William of Malmesbury,* ed. Reginald R. Darlington (London: Royal Historical Society, 1928). The translations are my own, but I have consulted J. H. F. Peile, *William of Malmesbury's Life of Saint Wulstan, Bishop of Worcester* (1934; reprint, Felinfact, Great Britain: Llanerch, 1996). The biographical sketch is based on Emma Mason, *St. Wulfstan of Worcester, c. 1008–1095* (Oxford: Basil Blackwell, 1990); my thanks to Ellen Martin for calling this book to my attention and locating a copy for me. I have also translated a prayer for guests from Wulfstan's prayer book, *The Portifolium of Saint Wul[f]stan,* ed. Anselm Hughes, Henry Bradshaw Society, nos. 89 and 90 (Leighton Buzzard, England: Henry Bradshaw Society, 1958–1960).

Permission Acknowledgments

Grateful acknowledgment is made to the following for permission to reprint previously published material:

Cistercian Publications for permission to quote from *The Life of Saint Pachomius and His Disciples,* translated by Armand Veilleux, O.C.S.O., *Pachomian Koinonia,* vol. 1, Cistercian Studies Series, no. 45. Copyright ©1980 by Cistercian Publications, Kalamazoo, MI, and Spencer, MS.

Doubleday, a division of Random House, Inc., for permission to quote from *Conjectures of a Guilty Bystander,* by Thomas Merton. Copyright ©1966 by The Abbey of Gethsemani.

Liturgical Press and Esther de Waal for permission to quote from *A Life-Giving Way: A Commentary on the Rule of St. Benedict,* by Esther de Waal. Copyright ©1995 by Liturgical Press, Collegeville, MN.

The Merton Legacy Trust for permission to quote from *Contemplation in a World of Action,* by Thomas Merton.

New Directions Publishing Corp. and Laurence Pollinger, Ltd., for permission to quote from *New Seeds of Contemplation,* by Thomas Merton. Copyright ©1961 by The Abbey of Gethsemani, Inc.

Paulist Press for permission to quote from *St. Athanasius,* translated and annotated by Robert T. Meyer, Ph.D. ©1950 by Rev. Johannes Quasten, Rev. Joseph C. Plumpe and Copyright ©1978 by Rev. Johannes Quasten and Rose Mary L. Plumpe.

Peregrina Press, Toronto, Ontario, Canada, for permission to quote from *The Life and Regimen of Blessed Syncletica* by Pseudo-Athanasius, translated by Elizabeth Bryson Bongie, Peregrina Translations Series, no. 1. Copyright ©1996.

SLG Press, Convent of the Incarnation, Fairacres, Oxford OX4 1TB, for permission to quote from *The Letters of Saint Antony the Great,* translated with an introduction by Derwas J. Chitty. Copyright ©1975 by The Community of the Sisters of the Love of God.

The Crossroad Publishing Company for permission to quote from *The Rule of Benedict,* by Sr. Joan Chittister. Copyright ©1992 by The Crossroad Publishing Company.

Other Essential Series Books
Available from Harper San Francisco:

Essential Confucius by Thomas Cleary

Essential Gay Mystics by Andrew Harvey

Essential Kabbalah by Daniel C. Matt

Essential Koran by Thomas Cleary

Essential Mystics by Andrew Harvey

Essential Rumi by Coleman Barks

Essential Sufism by James Fadiman and Robert Frager

Essential Tao by Thomas Cleary

Essential Tibetan Buddhism by Robert A. F. Thurman

Essential Zen by Kazuaki Tanahashi and Tensho David Schneider